Tragedy to Grace

TRAGEDY to *Grace*

A personal history
of perseverance and growth
through God.

DANIEL S. POKORNEY

trillium
memory
books

2018

Printed in the United States of America

First Edition: September 2018

ISBN 978-1-946970-95-4

Library of Congress Control Number: 2018956426

Published by
Trillium Memory Books
An imprint of redbat books
La Grande, OR 97850
www.trilliummemorybooks.com

Text set in Times

Cover design by
Nancy Allen

Book design by
Kristin Summers, redbat design | www.redbatdesign.com

DEDICATIONS

This book is dedicated to everyone who is beset by tragedy and wonders how they will get through the troubled times. God is with you and he will give you His grace if you trust in Him. Listen and wait for God's strength to come to you. The author also dedicates this book to each of his loved ones who has gone to eternal rest. Each of them touched my heart and they remain there to guide me back to that great reunion in heaven.

TABLE OF CONTENTS

AUTHOR'S PREFACE

The predominant feature of the cover of this book is a picture that I took of the roadside sign that marks the site of the accident that took the lives of four members of my family. The sign represents the tragedy that happened on Highway 14/16 in Northeastern Wyoming. The State of Wyoming graciously installs these signs, upon request, as a memorial and a reminder of an accident that took a life or lives. The sign remains in place for five years. I requested the sign in 2016. The actual highway is highlighted on the left side of the sign. The sun on the left of the picture is a representation of God's grace. The grassland is a representation of the loneliness that can envelop a person when a tragedy occurs. The grass however is still growing and being used as feed for livestock, therefore the land is still producing and is alive. When a tragedy falls on us, we must stay alive and grow in the grace that God will deliver.

The back cover is a collage of pictures of some of the people I have lost in my life. The top photo backdrop is my Grandpa and Grandma Stickney's farm in Nebraska. The bottom photo is a panoramic photo of the Grande Ronde Valley in Oregon. The inset pictures are: top left William Pokorney and William Pokorney Jr. Top right Ruby Jeanne Pokorney and Thomas Pokorney. Bottom left Sherman Stickney, Paul Miigerl, and Nellie Stickney. Bottom right Linda Pokorney and Diedra Pokorney.

All people referenced by name in the book have been contacted for permission to use their names, or they are deceased.

CHAPTER 1

A FINALITY ... OR IS IT?

It was the second Wednesday of January, 2015. I am about to call to order the final meeting that I will preside over as the Mayor of La Grande, Oregon. This would be my last official meeting in a community service career that included over forty years of volunteer activities in church, schools, and community. Within that forty years were sixteen years of elected service to the community.

Amazingly, I was not anxious about this moment. I was, contrary to my normal emotions, at peace with the decision to retire from elected service forever. To understand why I was not anxious, you need to know my normal personal demeanor for meetings. No matter how hard I prepared, I was always nervous, and I just about drove the city manager and city recorder to distraction because I wanted each meeting to run smoothly. I worked closely with the city manager and his staff to make sure I knew each and every action item. I made sure I knew the correct pronunciations of all names of people that would be presenting or that I would be appointing to city committees. The La Grande City Council was very visible to the public. We provided an inviting atmosphere for people to attend the meetings and give their input. The La Grande City Council meetings were broadcast by live feed on a cable-access channel and there were other media present in council chambers. I always tried to make presenters feel at ease and to not be nervous addressing the City Council. I never wanted to mis-speak or make a blunder that would reflect badly on the City of La Grande. This last meeting, my confidence was high, and my heart and mind had God in charge.

How can it be that my heart and mind are at ease? I left the office of Mayor with a solid approval of my performance within the community. I was still energetic and there were challenges that I would like to "see through" for the community. Overriding all of this however, was a deep-seated belief that elected public service should not be a career. The founding fathers wrote the Constitution of these United States of America with (I believe) the idea and goal was to have a citizen government. That government, at all levels, would have elected citizens represent their friends and neighbors for a pre-determined time, then that person would step aside and let another citizen take up the task.

There were however, other reasons and life directions that came into play. Four years earlier, I had made the decision that if elected by my fellow citizens, I would serve two, two-year terms, then step away. I made this decision public knowledge, but some thought that I would not serve more than one term because I would not be able to do the job. There were others who believed in my dream that the Mayor position could be effective if the right person were a listener and would speak for all the citizens. Although the form of government that La Grande used did not give the mayor many options to make individual decisions. I believed in using the office of mayor differently than it had been used. I believed I could be a leader by becoming visible and accessible to everyone. Through hard work and dedication, I became the kind of mayor that I had envisioned. God's hand would shine through however, as the ultimate deciding factor in my leaving public office.

In March of 2014, I had to decide to run again, or hold to my originally stated plan. I had many people pulling on me to continue to serve. Deep in my heart however, God was telling me that this time of my life was going to end. Somehow, that was very clear to me and I was at complete peace with the decision. So, the day of decision came and went with God in charge and leading as to His plan.

The final meeting was actually two different meetings. The outgoing mayor and council would do the normal opening sequence of the meeting and would discuss and vote on two "unfinished" items. Before the final "unfinished" items were discussed, there was a presentation of plaques to outgoing council members and myself. My plaque was tastefully simple. There was a gavel attached and an inscription that thanked me for my service and dedication to the citizens as Mayor. When the outgoing council finished the business at hand, I then commented that we would now perform the time-honored practice of an orderly transition of power. I introduced the new mayor and had him come forward. We shook hands and I wished him and the new council good luck in their work. I handed him the gavel and he immediately called the meeting to recess so as to allow for the seating of the new council. I gathered my briefcase and plaque, shook many hands of congratulations and thanks, and drove home. On the one-mile drive home, I cried tears of accomplishment.

I worked extremely hard in the four years I served as Mayor of La Grande. I attended over 650 meetings plus countless person to person contacts from the grocery store to the coffee shop. I attended city meetings, school meetings, and almost every public event held in the community. I was in all the parades, helped at the ribbon cuttings for new businesses, and made myself available for any community event. All this was done for no pay, and I held down a full-time job the entire time. Many days I would get off my job at 3:30 p.m. and have as many as three meetings between 3:30 p.m. and 8:30 p.m.

I have always been an emotional man. Tears come easy to me and many emotions can cause the waterworks to flow. Once I got home and dressed down, I sat in the dark, all alone,

and reflected on my time as Mayor. On the night I was elected, I fell to my knees in my living room and prayed for the
wisdom to lead the City of La Grande. God did not desert me
then, now I knelt in prayer to God for the wisdom and patience
to follow whatever path he had for my future. Wow! What a
path he chose.

CHAPTER 2

THE LEGACY THAT FORMED
MY LIFE MISSION

I now will present my life in a semi-orderly chronological manner. I will from time to time refer back and forth to events and times in my life, in order to give context. All the names in this book are the real names and places. I use the names of deceased family and friends in order to honor their memory. Those mentioned who are living, I have permission to reference them by name. To all others, I will beg forgiveness if they are hurt in any manner.

My home state of Nebraska is an amazing place. It is primarily a farming and ranching state, and since 1960 I was intimately involved in those noble pursuits. There is a national forest at Halsey, Nebraska. Amazingly, later in my life I would work in the wood products industry. The rich farm land and temperate climate is wonderfully suited to grow corn, soybeans, and alfalfa. The largest underground aquifer in the world (the Ogallala) supplies the massive amount of water needed for the crops and the population. The farm where I was raised used water from the great aquifer and I studied its positive effects on the people and economy of Nebraska. There are many rivers in the state. The Platte, which runs from the West boundary to the East boundary, where it empties into the massive Missouri River. The Loup River which starts as three forks eventually emptying into the Platte near Columbus, Nebraska. The farmers and ranchers (of which our family was one) are true environmental stewards of the land, water, and air quality. The raising of livestock is important to Nebraska and the nation. The Omaha Stockyards are one of the largest in the nation handling cattle, hogs, and sheep.

Nebraska's form of government is unique in the United States. It is a unicameral legislature, which means that there is just one legislative body made up of elected representatives from each region of the state. Early in my education, students were made aware of the uniqueness of the unicameral system. Higher education in Nebraska is led by The University of Nebraska. I was fortunate to attend this great center of learning, however because of my immaturity I did not take full advantage of the expertise of the instruction offered. Its three campuses in the state lead the nation in innovation in many areas. From agriculture research, to medical advancements, to educating new teachers, the institution is a very important land-grant university. I have been a fan of The University of Nebraska Cornhuskers Football Team since 1962. You see, Nebraska has zero professional sports teams and the Cornhusker football team elicits a following that borders on a religious experience. On Saturdays in the fall in the 1960s, as well as today, all radios were tuned to the Cornhusker football game. No matter what we were working on, the radio, if possible, was in close proximity so we could listen to the game. When I attended the university for the fall semester in 1972, I had a student ticket for all the Cornhusker home games that season. At that time Memorial Stadium held 67,000 fans, and on game day it was the third largest population center in the entire State of Nebraska. The Cornhusker fans are known as some of the most courteous fans in college football. We welcome the opponent and treat them with respect, win or lose.

It is the people, however, who make Nebraska the treasure that it is. The State of Nebraska leads the nation in family owned farms, with many ownerships going back three and four generations. The perseverance and grit that the people exhibit is a thing of beauty. With the many weather-related problems that beset Nebraska, the people roll with the punches and stay the course. Blizzards, hailstorms, floods, or tornados do not overwhelm the people: they just steel their resolve to go forward to better times. I have been caught in and been a victim of the severe weather that can happen in Nebraska.

A time-honored practice in Nebraska is the "finger wave."

On roads in Nebraska, when two vehicles meet, there is the finger wave between the drivers. Most drivers in Nebraska drive with on hand on the top of the steering wheel. When vehicles meet, the index finger is raised in a friendly gesture and acknowledgment between the drivers. I saw the finger wave as a small child and when I was old enough to drive, I assumed the "finger wave." When I visit and drive very long in Nebraska, I will find myself doing this gesture to other drivers. This is the root-stock I came from. If I can show and pass on one iota of that pioneer spirit to my descendants, then I will have carried on the legacy that is Nebraska.

The pioneers that came to settle the West often traveled through Nebraska. The Oregon Trail, The Mormon Trail, and the Gold Rush all used and endured the Nebraska land and climate in order to settle in the expansive western United States. Starting when I was around the age of ten years old, our family would visit the historic sites of the Pony Express, the Oregon Trail, and the Union Pacific Railroad. The pioneers had a large role in settling the West and dramatically increased the habitation of western Nebraska. The Nebraska Tourism Commission in the 1960s had as its motto: "Where the West Began." That motto was and is so true.

There are 253 cities, towns, and villages in Nebraska. Only four of them are over 50,000 population and only sixteen are 10,000 or more. The rest are very small towns and villages with that unique "small town" atmosphere. I grew up in and around these small towns and can attest to the local charm and pride that each of them proudly has and shows. In times of weather-related disasters or personal difficulties, the people rally with and for each other. I have seen and been a part of barn raisings, harvest bees, numerous other community pride builders. When I was sixteen years old, I remember one neighbor whose garage had caught fire and it looked like the volunteer firemen would not be able to contain it and keep it away from the home because of the wind and dry conditions. This was a close neighbor and there was no need for an invitation to help. About twenty of us neighbors literally carried all the furniture and possessions out of the house in order to preserve them. Fortunately, the firemen were able to contain the fire and we put everything back in the house before leaving. That, my friends, is community. That sense of community would raise its head many more times to me and some of those stories you will read later.

CHAPTER 3

BIRTH TO 6 YEARS OLD

It was Thursday February 4, 1954, when a loving couple became my earthly father and mother. I do not know the details of the pregnancy and birth, only that William and Ruby Jeanne Pokorney agreed early on that the name of this new baby would be Daniel if it was a boy. From this point on I will refer to my parents as most people knew them, Bill and Jeanne. I joined two older brothers. David, age three and Thomas, age two. My parents wanted their children to have names that reflected their strong dedication to the Bible. My name, Daniel, means judge. I wonder what my biblical name would have been if I would have been a girl?

I must have shown some patience, which is not my strongest attribute, as I was born in Grand Island, Nebraska, thirty-two miles from where I lived. According to my baby pictures I was a happy little guy. I even have one picture with my underpants on my head. (Oh My.) I am sure that I followed my big brothers around when I could and learned the "lay of the land." I faintly remember having ear infections and going 20 miles to a specialist. He must have done a good job, as I have excellent hearing to this day.

My grandparents, Sherman and Nellie Stickney, lived on a farm near Ravenna, Nebraska. My mother was their only child and these great people would become the most important influences in my life. (More on that tie-in later.) They mainly lived in the basement of the house because it was cooler in the summer and warmer in the winter. We visited the farm a lot and I will share many more recollections of those times later in the book. An added bonus of living in a basement house was the protection from the severe storms that are prevalent in that area of the Midwest.

We lived in the town of Ravenna, Nebraska, as my dad worked in a clothing store there. My dad was active in the community as a volunteer fireman, a football referee, and a Master Mason in the Masonic Lodge. My dad and mom were active in the Order of the Eastern Star and the Methodist Church. The town of Ravenna had a yearly festival called Annevar, which is Ravenna spelled backwards. The Annevar celebration dates back to 1887. It was a time for farm, ranch, and town to come together and celebrate. There were two parades during Annevar. My mother was very innovative in planning the Pokorney family's Children's Parade entry that all of us boys took part in.

My earliest memory has been questioned by some folks, but I stand by it because my mind's eye sees it so clearly. My Great Grandmother Zoucha lived for a time with my grandparents, and I remember her being assisted down the open basement stairway of the house on the farm. The name Zoucha is my Grandma Stickney's maiden name and is 100 percent Polish. I was, and I am still able to describe her very old-fashioned dress and high top laced shoes. Her hair was partially grey, and she could only walk with assistance. All of these details seems to lend credence to my memory. The part that is problematic for some to grasp is the fact that my Great Grandmother Zoucha was confined to a rest home in 1956. That means I would have to remember that scene at two years of age. I will stand by my memory of that day until I am proven wrong.

I remember that my grandparent's farm was like an eternal field trip. There was fishing at two different ponds and going after the big channel catfish in the South Loup river which bordered the farm. There were also snapping turtles, frogs, small animals of all kinds to amuse us youngsters. We ate the turtles (they are great as soup) and frog legs which are very good. Nothing went to waste and we learned to respect the prey. Many times, the fishing expeditions were family and multi-family events. Food brought by the ladies would be enjoyed by a big bonfire and we boys would try to catch the biggest and the most fish. In the farm ponds there were bullheads, carp, and bluegill fish. The smallest children (usually me or a cousin) first used a cane pole to fish, as a rod and reel were a little too complicated. When I graduated to the rod and open reel I quickly learned how to cast without causing a backlash in my reel. I have untangled so many fish lines that I am very good at it and enjoy the task even to this day. One day while fishing, I was stung on the wrist by a yellow jacket. I was crying and carrying-on, so my Uncle George took a chunk of chew out of his mouth and put it on the sting. The pain went away immediately but I kept the chew on there for quite a while thinking the pain would come back if I took it off. Those old remedies really do work.

The cows on the farm were always exciting for a little guy. The cows and bulls seemed so big that I was always afraid of them. In the spring the baby calves were more my size and I felt a certain kinship with them. As that herd of registered Herefords would go to water, they all walked in single file down a cow path. What a beautiful site that was. The animal kingdom, and cattle in particular, have natural leaders just like humans do. When it came time to go to water or move from pasture to pasture, there were always one or two old cows that would be the leaders of the herd. Later, I would come to see these beautiful animals in a different light. I would later see that they were an integral cog in the operation of the Stickney farm.

At about the age of three or four my parents built a new brick home in Ravenna. It was a one-story house with a daylight basement that faced east. The living room had a sunken floor and a huge fireplace. I have pictures of the family at Easter and Christmas time in front of that wonderful full-wall brick fireplace. My memories are sketchy in regard to the building process, except that the contractor/brick-layer said something that has stuck with me all these many years and miles. His name was Earl Wagner and he was a character. I am not sure how the conversation started, but we kids were eating raisins, and he said that those were really bugs. I still like and eat raisins, but always remember Mr. Wagner telling that funny tall tale.

Bill and Jeanne had a cadre of young people like themselves in Ravenna. Some of them had been classmates, as both Bill and Jeanne graduated from Ravenna High School. These young couples had a wide variety of occupations and were the up-and-coming leaders in a community of around 1,400 residents. They all had children and when they weren't working, they recreated together. Church activities, picnicking, fishing, and dancing were many of the family fun things enjoyed by these young couples. My Dad and two friends were high school football referees and they worked a game every Friday night during the season.

Many other memories come to me about this time in my life. Our big extended families had many family reunions. Sometimes they were planned around weddings, anniversaries, or funerals. The interactions with some cousins close to my age was great, but I remember the food and the fact that we usually traveled to different places (parks) for these reunions. When I was two years old, my brother Billy was born. I don't have a lot of memories of that time, except that I wasn't the baby anymore. Billy's arrival would complete this beautiful family: Dad, Mom, and four rambunctious boys. We were only in the new brick house for about a year when my Dad's boss, Mr. Max Warrick, bought another clothing store in Broken Bow, Nebraska. He asked my Dad to become the manager of that store. The Warrick's Clothing store was where my Dad worked in Ravenna and I guess Mr. Warrick liked his work. Broken Bow was about 50 miles west of Ravenna on Highway 2. Evidently the commute was too far so Bill, Jeanne, David, Thomas, myself, and Billy moved to Broken Bow.

We lived in a couple of locations before settling into a home in the northwest corner of Broken Bow. It was an interesting house with a circular drive, and the front of the house had a second-story veranda that was accessible from the master bedroom. On the west side of the house, there was a screened in sun porch/patio. It was called a Florida Room and I remember my mom and Grandma Stickney really liking the room. We were the last house before the open pasture country. Broken Bow was the beginning of the Nebraska Sandhills. We had many relatives living in western Nebraska, so we often visited the area. The world-famous grass prairie encompassed one quarter of the State of Nebraska. The Sandhills were the premier place for grazing and raising of grass hay in the United States. Over 500,000 beef cattle called the Sandhills home and it was not unusual to see cattle grazing in pastures with grass touching the underside of their bellies. There was open space behind the house and big cottonwood trees all the way around the house. In the open space, we had a marble ring for shooting marbles, and a full-size baseball field. My Grandpa Stickney made a tire swing, that hung from one of the big trees. The three older boys, plus neighbors, would see how high we could swing. We would also have someone wind up the swing as much as possible, then let it go and we would spin wildly, causing a dizzy rider and ringing laughter.

The Warrick's Clothing store in Broken Bow sold clothing, shoes, and finery for the whole family. My dad was meticulous in his work ethic and customer service. In the summer time, when it was very hot, my dad would come home at noon and shower and put on clean, pressed clothes. He was very conscience about his appearance and never wanted to look disheveled or have a possibility of body odor. The store was on the east side of the town square. Many communities in Nebraska have town squares and the town builds around the square. Some towns had the courthouse in the square, but Broken Bow had a large gazebo and a lot of green grass for public spaces. The town square was about one block square. The most desirable business locations were directly across from the town square.

At home, my mom was busy with four boys ranging in age from two to nine years of age. She still had time to give piano lessons and be a den mother for a Cub Scout group. My dad spent as much time with us as possible playing ball and such. I remember that every Friday night my dad would sit in his easy chair and watch the "Gillette Friday Night Fights." He always had a beer, poured it in a tall glass, and he put salt in it.

Several Christmas memories flood my mind. An article was written in the newspaper describing one of the family traditions that my mom started. We had a nativity scene that had a manger and 15 individual figurines. The manger was set up and the pieces were all individually wrapped in newspaper in the box. Each member of the family took turns choosing a wrapped figure, unwrapping it, and putting it in its correct place in and around the manger. The person that got the Baby Jesus was then entitled to open the first gift of Christmas. My family carry on this tradition to this day and I use the very same Nativity Scene that was purchased by Dad and Mom in 1948.

We celebrated our last Christmas together (1959) at our house in Broken Bow. Grandpa and Grandma Stickney came also. After the opening of gifts, there was a lot of wrapping paper, boxes, and such. My dad and Grandpa Stickney went out to the burn barrel to burn the remains of Christmas morning, and after the job was done, Grandma Stickney said that she could not find the ring that Grandpa Stickney had given her that day to commemorate their 30th wedding anniversary. After the ashes cooled, the ashes were sifted through and, sure enough, the burned ring was there. Grandpa Stickney later bought her another identical ring. It was silver setting with a ruby stone. Grandma Stickney wore that ring until her death in 2005.

These are the memories that I can muster that precede that fateful day of July 18, 1960. The next chapter will detail the days leading up to that day and the aftermath. What follows is a story of extreme tragedy but yet God's hands and grace will be evident. It also is the moment that I believe I was transformed into the man I became. I cannot be sure of that fact, but given the enormity of the situation, it at least gave me a life that I very likely would not have had.

CHAPTER 4

BAD THINGS HAPPEN
TO GOOD PEOPLE

In the spring of 1960 the Stickneys and the Pokorneys were planning a vacation trip that had many facets. Sherman and Nellie Stickney were farming near Ravenna. They had 620 acres of tillable farmland and pasture. The entire eastern boundary was the South Loup River. They grew corn and alfalfa. They ran about 85 head of registered Hereford cattle and had about thirty to forty head of two-year-old feeder cattle in the feedlot. The Stickneys were active in their church, the Masonic Lodge, and Order of the Eastern Star. Jeanne was their only child and she was married with children. Grandpa and Grandma Stickney were running a very busy farm by themselves. With the business of farming, the work was never done. They tilled the land and irrigated the corn, loose-stacked alfalfa hay, tended to the livestock. Along with that, they still had the housework and all other farm and ranch duties.

The Pokorneys were busy with Bill managing the clothing store, while Jeanne was raising the four boys. The family was active in church and school. The two older boys were in the Cub Scouts. Both Bill and Jeanne had been active in the Masonic Lodge and Eastern Star when they lived in Ravenna, but their busy life in Broken Bow did not allow enough time to become active in those pursuits now.

The vacation plan called for Bill to pull a twelve-foot camp trailer behind the family's 1957 Buick Special. Sherman and Nellie Stickney would follow in their 1959 Chevrolet Biscayne. Bill's mother Sophia Pokorney would also travel with the two families. The combined group would travel to Yellowstone Park and enjoy a few days there. The Stickneys and Grandma Sophia Pokorney would then return to Ravenna and the six Pokorneys would go on to the Oregon Coast where many relatives lived. The Stickneys had arranged for friends and neighbors to watch the farm for a few days before they needed to get back. Grandma Pokorney was older than Grandpa and Grandma Stickney and could not withstand such a long trip all the way to the Pacific Coast. July was chosen because that was the best time for the farm. Cattle were in the pasture, corn was growing, and alfalfa was between cuttings. In order for there to be room for all to ride, two of the boys would take turns riding with the Stickneys. At each meal stop or night stop the boys would change vehicles. I do not remember how it was determined who rode with Grandpa and Grandma Stickney, but I remember it being an intense time with much pleading and begging. The "winners" got to ride with Grandpa and Grandma Stickney.

We departed our homes and I have no memory until we got to the Black Hills and saw Mount Rushmore. I have photos from the old Brownie camera and the date is printed on the border of each photo. The pictures at Mount Rushmore read July 18, 1960. We were to drive to Sheridan, Wyoming that night, as we had relatives there. We stopped for dinner in Gillette, Wyoming. Meals were basically picnics out of the camp trailer. We had three great cooks along, so of course we did not go hungry. As we got ready to leave Gillette, the contest for the rides began. It was determined that my brother David and I would ride with Grandpa and Grandma Stickney until we stopped for the night. So, there were five people in the Pokorney car and four in Stickney car.

Wyoming Highway 14 runs between Gillette and Sheridan. It was open range area with cattle and lots of antelope. The ranches in that area were few and far between. About 30 miles from Gillette there was a little stopping place for gas and food called Spotted Horse, Wyoming. It was just two buildings and was really just a very small place. As we traveled through Spotted Horse, we were going straight West. The time was about 7:00 pm. From Spotted Horse we went down a hill and at the bottom of the hill there was Spotted Horse Creek. The bridge over the creek was narrow and the road was curving as it started up a hill. The Pokorney car and trailer led the way and the Stickney car followed. As the Pokorney vehicle started up the hill about three hundred yards, there was a terrible collision. I was riding with the Stickneys and we were about one-half mile behind the Pokorneys. We saw a terrific cloud of dust as we pulled up to the site. My Grandma Nellie screamed "Oh my God Sherman." I do not remember what I felt and I still only remember bits and pieces of what happened next. I was six years old at this time. My Grandpa Sherman told us to stay in the car while he went to the site. Of course, none of us obeyed and we all ran to the wreckage. The car was sitting on the road and smashed down. The top was completely gone, and the camp trailer was in a million pieces in the ditch. A farm truck was laying on its side and the wheels were turning. My dad was trapped in the driver's seat and was calling for help. My brother David and I stood by him, and I guess we thought we could help him. The car was so smashed down I was almost looking down at my dad and I was just a little guy. My Grandma Pokorney was standing up in the backseat calling for help. She looked like she was hardly injured at all. Sherman and Nellie evidently went to my mom and brothers. Like I said, my memories are sketchy. I was six years old and only remember my dad and Grandma Pokorney because they were alive. I have no recollection of my mom and brother Thomas who were killed instantly. Brother Billy and my dad were mortally wounded and lived several hours while we waited for help to arrive. I have no memory of Billy at this point either. Later in my life I talked to a psychologist who told me that my sub-conscious will not let me remember certain things, primarily because of my young age at the time. My brother David was ten years old and presumably remembers more than me. My brother David was interviewed for this book and told me that the facts I have presented are correct as per his memory. If he had or has additional memories, he did not share them with me.

This stretch of highway was very isolated and since this was 1960, medical help was 30 miles away. The road of course was blocked, and people were stopping to offer whatever help they could. With the medical advances of today, (Life Flight and such), my dad could have possibly been saved. He died from chest injuries from the steering wheel crushing him. My mom and two brothers died of head injuries. My Grandma Pokorney received only scratches and lived another twenty years. I talked to her before she died, and she said that she was very tired during the drive and had fallen asleep in the back seat. She survived because everything went over her very fast. The truck driver was a local rancher and recovered from his injuries but has since passed away. The vehicles had met headlight to headlight. Being higher and loaded down with lumber, the truck went over the big Buick. The bed of the farm truck extended out past the truck cab and it acted like a knife as it sheared off the roof of the car. The truck then smashed the trailer before ending up on its side back in its lane. I have been told that my Grandpa Stickney ran up the hill, about a half mile to the little store and bar called Spotted Horse, Wyoming. Imagine a fifty-one-year-old man, after seeing the carnage of his only daughter and family, running full tilt up hill to summon help.

After it was dark, my brother and I were taken to a nearby ranch house. This was probably done to get us away from the scene. Later we traveled to the hospital and we were there when they told us my dad and brother Billy had died.

In 2016 I went to the site and God was with me that day. I felt my family and also felt the power of God saying, "After fifty-six years, you now know all there is to know." I also communicated with the boy—now a man who took us into their home. He gave me additional information which was a blessing. I personally met the only remaining law enforcement officer alive who was at the scene. He also provided some information for me. The authorities in Campbell County, Wyoming were of the greatest help in my search for information and I thanked them all.

When I retired in 2016, I decided to research whatever I could find on the accident. Amazingly, I found almost all the documentation from the accident and subsequent investigation from Campbell County, Wyoming. The result of the investigation showed that my dad had crossed the center line of the highway by about 8 inches. At the time of the accident, my dad was looking into a setting sun, and pulling an older camp trailer. My dad only had one eye. He had lost his left eye, because of a wood cutting accident as a child. He had just crossed a bridge that had a turn built into it. Do I blame my dad? No! Any one of those circumstances could have resulted in the accident, let alone all of them happening at once. Do I blame the truck driver? No! Do I blame God? No! I praise God for what happened after the accident.

An accident it truly was. Grief and despair would pull deep from the family left behind. A close knit small community would be shaken to its core, and yet that steady hand of God would gently give guidance. To those directly involved, the path forward would take twists and turns. I cannot and will not try to speak for anyone else about how a moment in time, changed so many lives. No one left would have an easy road.

Many years later, I would ask myself a question that has many answers. As the boys clamored for the chance to ride with Grandpa and Grandma Stickney and the decision was made, did I win or lose? I contend I did both. My life as I knew it certainly had been changed, yet I cannot imagine having a better family and community to rescue my brother and me. They all did their best to see that there would be no other victims from this accident. There are many times in our lives that when events happen to us, good or bad, we try to rationalize the impact on us. Truly, only God knows the ultimate impact of events on our lives, and I believe if we wait for His guidance,

He will provide the best possible outcome.

This would be the first tragedy of many in my life. To keep with the theme of this book, the grace that followed, was that God saw to it that Grandpa and Grandma Stickney would take in my brother and me and give us a normal, although somewhat different, life. God also blessed me as to not blame anyone for what had happened, nor hold animosity towards anyone for this big change in my life, and to be open to learning a work ethic that would serve me well many facets of my life.

CHAPTER 5

AFTERMATH—WHERE AND HOW DO WE START?

Again, my memories fade in and out during this time. I remember being very scared on the drive back to Nebraska. Knowing what I know now, I imagine the logistics that my Grandpa Sherm had to deal with were huge. Funeral arrangements for four family members in our small community would come first. Amazingly, Grandpa Sherm bought sixteen plots in the new part of the Highland Park Cemetery in Ravenna. All the plots were together in two rows; eight in each row and right by an entrance and close to the county road. He did this, so we would all be together in perpetuity.

Family came from all over the country and I remember so many people being around. The funeral was held in the Ravenna High School auditorium because it was the only facility that could accommodate the expected huge attendance. The four caskets were sitting on the floor in front of the stage. Dad and mom in the middle and Tommy and Billy on each side. Each casket had beautiful flowers on it: The entire floor in front of the stage and the stage itself were crowded with flowers of all kinds. Reverend Jacobson, the family's pastor at the Methodist Church, gave a thoughtful and insightful address. The comforting words of Rev. Jacobson were so highly thought of that the Ravenna News, the local newspaper, printed his entire funeral sermon the week after the funeral. The attendance was over 700 people. It was and is the largest funeral ever held in Ravenna, Nebraska.

I do not remember if I grieved or how intense my grief was. I certainly remember my Grandpa and Grandma Stickney grieving tremendously. One night, (I do not know how long after the accident), I woke up with a terrible feeling that my Grandpa Sherm had died. I laid awake in my bed for what seemed like an eternity, then walked to my grandpa and grandma's bedroom. When I heard my Grandpa Sherm snoring, I knew that everything was okay. I have never told anyone this story, but I believe that the nightmare came from my sub-conscious. I believe that I feared losing another person who was taking care of me. Other than the pain of the memories that come to me now, that I am in my 'golden years', I do not feel that I suffered from any long-standing mental impairments from this most life-shattering event. On the contrary, I believe with all my heart that God used this time in my young life to try me and refine me for the road ahead. God, later in my life, would test my fear of losing loved ones—to a high level.

I do know that when I was about thirty years old I had a period of rather intense grieving. I had many questions that I had never asked and needed some answers. Grandpa and Grandma Stickney were still alive, but I felt that if I asked specific questions I would bring up the hurt in them all over again. The hurt always seemed to be close to them. I heard later that there was concern among friends and family that those wonderful people (my Grandpa and Grandma Stickney), would not be able to withstand the loss and grief. So, on the advice of friends and my wife, I let those feelings subside. When God was ready, or thought I was ready, He would lead me down the path to discovery.

They had so many responsibilities to take care of plus still operate the farm. Many family, friends, and neighbors helped with the different tasks. There was a house and possessions to liquidate and the estate of my parents to settle. I do not remember being told what would happen to my brother David and me. I guess it again was a grace that I was so young that all the worrisome and stressful time is non-existent to me. Even though the memories cannot be brought to light in a cognitive way, I do believe that everything I witnessed was and is stored in a sub-conscious part of my mind. God allows me to actually remember some details, but He has reserved other details for the strength of my character. I would not be surprised to find that I have, during my life, put into practice many things that I learned and do not remember learning them.

I just remember that at some point, my brother David and I were told that we were going to live with Grandpa and Grandma Stickney on the farm permanently. I remember thinking that it would be just like each time when we visited before the accident. Soon though, we learned that we would be needed to work on the farm. They became our legal guardians as there was really not anyone else. My dad's siblings were older or not settled and my Grandma Pokorney was too old to care for two young boys. Perhaps the most amazing fact is that Grandpa and Grandma Stickney thought so much of protecting our identity as Pokorneys, they became our guardians instead of adopting my brother and me. The guardianship was not easy for them and they had to adhere to very strict guidelines as administered by the courts. The Stickneys lived the frugal life like many farm families of that time. Adding the care of two young boys could not have been easy for them. A further testament to the character of my grandparents, Sherman and Nellie Stickney, is the fact that every cent of the SSI payments that my brother and I received, from 1960 until we were eighteen years old, was saved for us and given to us when we were of age. That is sacrifice, caring, and love to the highest degree.

CHAPTER 6

STARTING A DIFFERENT LIFE

The accident happened on July 18, 1960, and with everything going on, my brother David and I started school in August in the little village of Poole, Nebraska. In Poole there was a big brick building that served as the school for rural students grades one through eight. We knew no one at the school but felt accepted as if we had been there all our lives. The school building had a full basement, a full kitchen, and a full stage for plays and such. The stage even had a trap door built into the floor. I will never forget that the curtain of the stage rolled up on a very heavy steel roller. When the curtain would raise, the roller would roll up the canvas curtain from the floor. The raised curtain around the heavy roller had to be secured really good because if it dropped it would severely injure someone. Outside the school, there was a three to four-acre playground that had a full baseball diamond, a flat play area for running games, and playground equipment.

We only lived about three miles from the school, as the crow flies, but the only good road was about six miles driving distance. The school had a regular school bus for the majority of the students. They all lived south of the village and school. North of the village and school there were six students. A local family provided and drove a 1952 Chevrolet sedan for the transportation of the north students. My brother David and I walked a quarter mile driveway each day to catch the car/bus, then walked the same road back after school: four children in the back and two in the front seat with the driver. There were no seat belts in the car and by God's grace there were no injuries. They drove that old car in all kinds of weather and I do not remember tire chains ever being used. There were some very severe winter days and (Oh yes,) the roads were all gravel.

The Luce family was the entire support staff of the Poole School. Cliff drove the big bus and was the janitor/groundkeeper. Leora was the cook and she always made very nutritious food. They lived right next door to the school and were always available.

Each teacher taught several grades. Grades one, two, and three, were the "Lower" room. Grades four, five, and six were in "Middle" room and grades seven and eight in the "Upper" room.

Times were different then and at Poole School we had a health check at the beginning of the school day. A student was assigned the duty of checking fellow student's fingernails for dirt, teeth for brushing, and hair for combing. Two students

from the "Middle" room carried the folded United States flag
out to the flag pole and properly raised the flag. At the end of
the day the flag-duty students would go out and lower the flag
and fold it correctly. The proper care of the United States flag
was very important to the families and community. The training of the unfolding, raising, lowering, and folding the flag
again was treated as a privilege and civic duty. We also learned
our nations historical documents and all the patriotic songs.

The teachers were very strict and corporal punishment was
the norm. A rap on the knuckles, sitting in the corner while
facing the corner, and a swat on the rear were not out of the
ordinary. One instance in fourth grade has had a lasting impact
on me. We were instructed to draw an action picture. I chose
a goose flying in the air. I made a good body of the goose and
had the one wing drawn. I figured that both wings needed to be
seen, so I drew a wing on the far side of the goose and had it
come all the way around the top of the goose, so it was beside
the other wing. I realized that it did not look right, but I handed it in anyway. The teacher, who shall remain nameless, was
showing the pictures to the class, one by one. When she got to
mine, she laughed and said, "Isn't this the silliest picture." To
this day I cannot and will not attempt artwork.

I remember being in school on November 22, 1963 when
the custodian came in to tell us that President Kennedy had
been killed. As a nine year old, I was not aware of the impact
on people and the country. I remember the teacher weeping

and to the students that was certainly a sign that the event was very important.

One of the fun events that occurred was—in the early 1960s the major league baseball World Series games were played in the daytime and we were allowed to listen to the World Series games in 1964 when the St. Louis Cardinals defeated the New York Yankees.

Recess time was a time for the boys to show our athletic abilities. We had running games like "Pump Pump Pull Away," "Red Rover Red Rover," and others. We played "Ante Ante Over" with a ball over the bus barn. I was never the best player of the games, but I could run fast enough to be competitive.

David and I began to take piano lessons and we received training from several different teachers over the next five years. Grandpa and Grandma purchased a brand-new piano and we enjoyed learning to play. We had recitals and I guess the performer in me really liked those times. That beautiful piano stayed with me through the big move to Oregon and I finally donated it in 2002. It was still in excellent condition and I hope that it is still giving enjoyment to whoever is playing it. I also took accordion lessons, which I really enjoyed. Learning the instruments and music gave me a sense of accomplishment. The ability to play the music was also enjoyable to my grandparents because my mother had been a piano player and teacher.

Until 1965 Nebraska had several hundred school districts, then there was a massive school re-districting in the state.

Poole and many surrounding little districts were closed and absorbed into the Ravenna School District. At the beginning of the 1965-66 school year, I was bused about six miles into the town of Ravenna to start seventh grade.

CHAPTER 7

GOING TO "TOWN SCHOOL"

Going to the big school in Ravenna was traumatic for the children from the outlying districts who were re-districted into one big school district— at least it seemed big at the time. All students in grades seven through twelve were in one building. The total number of students was approximately two-hundred compared to the forty total students at the Poole School. The building was all white and it was the same building where my family's funeral was held. It had an inscription carved into the side of the building, that said: "Dedicated to all veterans who had served." Strangely, I felt a sense of closeness with that school building because it was the site of funeral of my family.

I started in the seventh grade and my brother was in the tenth grade. The classes were held in different rooms and I had to learn the layout of the school and to manage the travel time between classes. The students from the small country school like myself had a harder time adjusting to the hustle and bustle of the "big school." For the first time we were both exposed to organized sports at the school level. We were also exposed to many different children and new freedoms. There were times when the temptation was great and the perceived need to "fit in" became a problem. During this time, I was exposed to smoking. I found it a terrible thing to do, it made me sick, and I have never done it since. Starting in seventh grade I did make many good friends. I went to school with these friends for six years and we have remained friends for these many, many years. My best friend was Duane Betke. We practiced sports together and that practice on our own made us better when it came to the school sports. Duane was a very good basketball player and I tried to play up to his level. He was such a good friend that he was both my wife and my choice to be my son's godfather.

I was not the best student because I was easily distracted. I was a very social person and many times played the class clown. Every report said the same thing: "If Dan would apply himself, he could be a very good student." I was the recipient of many interesting forms of discipline. In shop class, I would have to stand on my tiptoes with my nose on a dot on the wall. Sometimes I had to stay after school to sand wooden desks that I had carved or written on.

There was an open campus and sometimes my friends and I would walk the four blocks to downtown Ravenna and go to one of the local taverns to eat lunch and play the juke box. It was not illegal for minors to be in the taverns, but they could not be at the bar. There were chili dogs at the Cozy Tavern and pan-fried hamburgers at the Palace Tavern.

During my eighth-grade school year, the Ravenna School District built a new high school on the outskirts of town. My freshman class, the class of "1972", would be the first class to attend all four years of high school in a brand-new school. My brother David's class would be the last class to graduate from the stately old "white school."

Sometime in seventh grade, I became aware of a girl that had many of the same classes that I had. In almost every class, the students were seated alphabetically. I sat behind a girl who was tall for her age and had a bubbly personality. We both had come from one of the little out-of-town districts. Her last name began with "M" and mine with "P", so I sat behind her in classes. I wasn't too interested in girls at that point in my life, but there seemed to be just "something" about that girl named Linda. Later on, in this book, she will become a central figure in this life of mine.

CHAPTER 8

LEARNING THE FARM LIFE

The farm consisted of 620 acres. There was about 250 acres of tillable land and about 370 acres of pasture land. The eastern border was the South Loup River. The Loup is a sandy bottom river that flows through Nebraska in three tributaries. The other two Loup tributaries are the Middle and the North Loup. The river and backwater ponds were about one-quarter of a mile from the farmstead. The farm had the oldest water right on the South Loup. That meant we could and did use the river water for irrigation. There was a large backwater pond beside the river that had excellent fishing. The fields adjacent to the river were also sub-irrigated by the Loup. The tillable land was nearly flat while the pasture land was much hillier. The soil was sandy loam and, if the bare soil was blown by the wind, the sandy soil would become very fine and drift like snow.

My Grandpa and Grandma Stickney had lived on the farm since 1931 and had owned this farm since 1934. Together, they had made it a completely self-sufficient farm. That meant that the crops that were raised, corn and alfalfa hay, were sufficient to feed the cattle through the long winters without having to buy additional feed. Very little corn was sold as it was utilized on the farm. The sale of the cattle provided the primary income of the farm.

The first years on the farm were very hard on Sherman, Nellie and their little daughter Ruby Jeanne. The early 1930s were a time of economic depression and drought. The farm had very sandy soil that would blow and drift just like snow. The farming techniques that were used to strengthen the soil were to plant alfalfa which had very long roots, and practice crop rotation. The corn had to be put in the ground by listing. Listing, is a process by which the seed was planted in a furrow and there was a ridge on either side. This protected the small seedling until it was about twelve inches high. At that point, the plant had a better chance of survival in case of a wind storm that would blow the sand. When the sand was blowing, it could and would cut a small plant off at ground level. The soil was also improved by crop rotation. Alfalfa would be planted and harvested for about five years, then the alfalfa would be plowed under and corn would then be planted. The corn would not need as much fertilizer for the first few years because the alfalfa had put nitrogen into the soil naturally. In the first few years they raised just a few cattle and pigs. They had to control the number of offspring from the livestock because many times there was no feed for them due to the drought. You couldn't butcher many animals because there was very little refrigeration and no freezing capabilities. I remember stories of my Grandpa Sherm shooting hogs and leaving them for the scavengers because they could not afford to feed them or keep their meat.

In 1960 the cattle herd consisted of about eighty-five cow/calf pairs and thirty to thirty-five yearlings that were fattened to about 1000 pounds for market. There was also enough pasture for all the cattle with no need of renting further pasture. The cattle were registered Herefords. The cattle stayed in the pastures for most of the year. When winter came, they were all moved down to one of the corn fields that had been harvested and fed the alfalfa hay that had been raised. The fields where they stayed were surrounded by temporary electric fence. Some days when the snow and cold were especially bad, it was an all-day task to feed the cows. My grandfather would plow a road to the cows, feed them the hay, make sure they had access to water, and make his way back to the farmstead. I also did this process many times and it was time consuming, but necessary. The cows would have their calves in February and March and many times it would be necessary to help a cow deliver a calf. This was especially true with first calf heifers. It was an interesting experience for a youngster. The beautiful time of birth gave me a profound respect for life. The weather was usually cold and wet, and sometimes help was necessary for the life of the cow and calf. Grandpa Sherm and I would have to crawl to the cow (to avoid startling the cow) to assist with the calving process. We assisted by taking leather straps with a loop on one end and reaching inside the womb of the cow to put the loop around both front hoofs of the calf. A steady pulling motion combined with the cows natural pushing would ease the newborn calf from the mother.

The farmstead consisted of the house, which was added on to and remodeled in about 1963, a cement block barn, a machine shop, many other out-buildings, and three feedlots. The farmstead was one-quarter of a mile from the gravel road. The lane from the gravel road to the farmstead was a dirt road. It went through a pasture and across an earthen dam built in the 1950s for flood control, fishing, and stock water. There were two windmills, each with its own large stock tanks used to water the cattle. Windmills were a very efficient and free source of power to get the water from the ground to the cattle.

Grandpa Sherm only used John Deere tractors and all the row crop machinery was set up for two rows at a time. The alfalfa hay was mowed with sickle bar mowers, raked into windrows, and loose stacked in the field. In the fall some of the stacks were moved to the farmyard next to the feedlot for winter feed. One of the chores my brother David and I had was walking the top of the stacks and pitchforking down hay into feed bunks for the yearling cattle in the feedlot. The rest of the stacks were left in the field to feed to the stock cows during the winter.

Irrigation on the farm was done by sprinkler pipe until about 1963. At age six, I could already help move the irrigation pipe. The four-inch aluminum pipe would have a six-foot riser on one end and a rain bird sprinkler head attached to it. To move from location to location the pipe mover drained the pipe, then lifted it above the growing corn stalks and reattach it to the line. The pipe movers had to wear a long sleeve shirt that had been re-enforced with leather on the sleeves. The reason for that was because the corn leaves were so sharp, they would tear through regular material or your arms if they were exposed. Most of the tillable land was leveled in 1963 to allow for flood irrigation from gated pipe. The gated pipe was a huge advancement and allowed one person to do the irrigating. Approximately 100 acres was sub-irrigated. Sub-irrigation means that the crops received enough water from under the ground and needed no further irrigation. That land was the closest to the South Loup River that bordered the farm.

The corn was picked in the fall before the snows came and stored on the cob in corn cribs. Corn cribs were about 15 feet around and had a circular wood floor. Four-foot hog wire was shaped into a circle slightly smaller than the circular wood floor. As the corn was put into the wire ring and filled up, another wire ring was added. The corn cribs were four rings high and there were five total corn cribs. Once a year, usually in the spring, a neighbor who had a corn sheller would come and shell all the corn in the cribs. The corn sheller was a very big machine that the ears of corn went into and the corn kernels were shelled off the cob. The shelled corn was put in inside storage bins in the barn and machine shed. The corn kernels came out one spout and the cobs out the other. This operation was very labor intensive and took five or six men about two full days to complete. Everyone helped during this time, as there was plenty to do even for my brother David and me. This process was repeated at other neighboring farms, as the corn sheller served many farmers. Many friends and neighbors went to each farmstead to complete the task. The corn sheller was an expensive and large piece of machinery, therefore not all neighbors could afford one just for their own use. My Grandma Nellie would serve dinner and afternoon snack for all the working men when the corn sheller was at our farm.

Coming to the farm to live and work was a life-changing experience. My brother and I learned to help and handle tasks on the farm. We learned the proper use of tractors and machinery for the row crops and haying. We learned fence building and mending tasks. My Grandpa and Grandma Stickney were adamant that all things must be done right. Crop rows were straight, haystacks were well built and straight, and the cattle were not abused. Keeping the costs down on the farm was very important. Machinery was repaired instead of being replaced by new parts. Sometimes you had to buy a new part, but if you could repair it, then so much the better. Therefore, we learned to weld, overhaul engines, and work in the shop to keep everything working. We worked hard, and my Grandma Nellie saw to it that we ate well. Hundreds of chickens were raised for butchering. Some of the older hens were the egg layers and provided enough eggs for our use and even some to sell. There was a huge garden and the ground was spaded and raked by hand, in preparation of the planting. We butchered our own beef, pork, and game animals. Most of the food we ate was homemade. Bread, egg noodles, canned vegetables and meats, and desserts were just some of the fantastic food that Grandma Nellie would cook and serve with a loving heart.

David and I learned animal husbandry, which is learning about livestock and the proper way to take care of them. By doing this we learned to respect all animals, especially the cattle. They were the main source of income for the farm and we learned to help with calving, to keep them disease free, and to feed them properly, because they would eventually be sold for operating money. We loved the cattle and many times had names for them but could not become emotionally attached to them. We learned that the livestock were a renewable resource for the rancher and their life of service was five to ten years.

Not all the time on the farm was tedious and endless work. My brother David and I also learned to hunt, fish, and trap. We had whitetail deer on the property and we harvested one each year. The deer were quite destructive because they would run through and destroy fencing. We also hunted pheasants, quail, and rabbit for meat. We hunted other animals like coyote, raccoon, and assorted birds for predator control. Occasionally, we would hunt ducks and geese.

We fished in the Loup River for channel catfish, carp, and bullheads. In the summer time we would take several days and "run set lines." We would go down to the grass meadow beside the river and catch many green frogs for bait. We would use string with a big hook at the end and tie the string to a tree on the edge of the river, or we would use a stick on a sandbar as an anchor for the line. We would attach a frog to the hook and put it in the water. There would be about ten to fifteen lines in the water at one time. About every six hours, day and night, we would walk in the river to check the lines. We carried a gunny sack for the fish and a gunny sack that had more live frogs for bait. It was tiring but exhilarating for young boys to catch many big fish. We had to do everything ourselves including cleaning the fish. I guess this is why I still love fish, especially catfish.

Grandpa Sherm was an enthusiastic fisherman. He had the "patience of Job" when it came to fishing. If the fish were biting, he would keep trying for bigger fish. If the biting was slow, he would be forever optimistic that something would happen, and the fish would start biting. He never wasted fish. If the fish was small, he would be very careful to get the hook out in order to not hurt the fish and then he could release it. If the fish was injured too badly, he then kept the fish to eat.

The channel catfish were his favorite, but he also caught blue catfish and mud catfish. Later on, after he retired from the farm, he learned to fish for walleye pike, northern pike, white bass, and crappie. These types of fish were found in the reservoirs that we fished in. He took a special delight in learning to catch any kind of fish that he had not caught before. Before age caught up with him, he even tried his hand at salmon, trout, and surf fishing in the Pacific Ocean. He usually caught fish, but even if no fish were biting, he still relished the serenity of fishing and being outdoors.

Grandpa Sherm taught us how to trap animals along the river. He had trapped many years before and had the knowledge to pass on to us. We trapped muskrat, beaver, raccoon, and an occasional mink. We skinned the animals and took good care of the pelts. In the spring, a fur buyer would come to the farm and buy our furs. My brother and I got to keep the money we had earned. Trapping was very difficult to learn, and we certainly earned our money. The art of effective trapping involves the study of the prey's movements, strategic placing of the traps, and proper care of the hides.

David and I became proficient at rifle and shotgun shooting. Our Dad had passed down to us a matching set of Remington shotguns: 12-gauge, 20-gauge, and .410-gauge. A special memory of mine is one day when Grandpa Sherm and I were down by the river fixing fence and there was a chicken hawk sitting on the top of a haystack about two-hundred yards away. He told me to take a shot at the hawk, and if I missed, he would show me how it was done. Now, my Grandpa Sherm was an excellent marksman. I could probably count on one hand how many times I saw him miss anything with any gun. I steadied the Remington .22 bolt action rifle (no scope) on the hood of the pickup, and just as I was pulling the trigger, the hawk lifted off the haystack. I raised my sight just a little and pulled the trigger. The bird fell dead on the haystack. My Grandpa took his hat off and said, "I'll be damned." I do not think I could do that again.

An event happened one summer evening that will be forever etched in my memory. David and I were at the farm pond down by the river. There had been high water from a heavy rain and the South Loup River had overflowed into the farm pond adjacent to the river. When that happened, the big carp would escape the river and go into the grassy, marshy area of the pond. David and I had a King Neptune—style fish spear with a twelve-foot wood handle. Being thirteen years old, David would throw the fish spear from the bank and try to hit the big carp. The water was only about eight to ten inches deep and the grass was about ten to twelve inches high. When the carp would swim through the water and grass, we could see their backs. I was nine years old and when he hit one of the carp, I would walk out into the water to get the fish. I would then put the fish in a gunny sack on the bank and await the next kill. I was not allowed by David to throw the spear. After a while that evening, I became tired of doing all the work and I said, "I am going home." Home was a quarter mile away and, of course, we had walked down to the pond where the fish spearing was happening. David said that I could not leave until he was ready to leave. I started walking toward the farmstead and David said, "You better stop, or I will throw this spear at you." I kept walking and suddenly something hit the calf of my left leg. I looked down and saw the fish spear sticking out of my leg. I fell down crying. It hurt a lot and I imagine I was scared. David ran to me and upon seeing the spear in my leg, he panicked and reached down and pulled the spear out of my leg. Well the spear had gone in past the barb, so the size of the wound was made worse. I then became really scared. We wrapped David's shirt around my leg and made the slow one-quarter mile walk home. David was scared of getting into trouble for throwing the spear at me, so we made up a story about how I injured my leg. When Grandpa and Grandma Stickney came home, they doctored me and after a few days, the incident seemed to be forgotten. Many years later, Grandma Nellie told us that they had figured out what had happened but chose not to discipline David. To this day, I still have an indentation and scar on the calf of my left leg. I have had no ill effects from this event, but a life-long memory exists. David and I have talked about this time, and we basically agree about what happened. We differ on the fact of whether or not the intent was there to actually hit me with the spear.

CHAPTER 9

THE FAMILY CHANGES

In the summer of 1967 my brother David and his girlfriend conceived a child out of wedlock. David was going into his senior year at Ravenna High School and his girlfriend was going into her junior year. No family wants to go through a trying time like this, but both families came together and agreed that a marriage should take place. Before school started in the fall of 1967, the Ravenna School Board decided that neither David or his girlfriend would be allowed to attend school or be involved in any extra-circular activities. David was a stand-out athlete in three sports and this decision hit him hard. He did get tutoring at night and received his diploma in the spring of 1968. The punishment that was imposed at that time seem archaic by today's standards, but that was the way it was in that time and place.

I believe that the punishment put upon the two young people in this case was excessive. They were not the first high school students to conceive a child out-of-wedlock and they will not be the last. The punishment issued deeply affected both my brother David and his girlfriend. It affected both of them as to their education and self-esteem. The end result was just a vindictive swipe at two young people. The actions that the school board took did not create a deterrent or any kind of result that the school board must have envisioned it would. The punishment that was handed down by the school board had not been done before this incident, or after. Truly, the sad part is that it affected not only the lives of the two young people in this case, but also had long reaching ramifications within both families.

The baby was born in December and David and family left home and moved into a house. I was now the only one left at home, and I began to flourish in my education, personal interactions, and responsibilities on the farm. I count this as tragedy number two because I hated to see my brother be punished so severely. The grace that came from the tragedy was an awareness of how I should live my life so that I would not have to endure what my brother went through.

Many times, both good and bad examples of others in our lives, can influence a person. I truly believe that I was granted the grace to determine what path I should follow in my life. God has granted me freewill and although I have strayed from the path, I have always come back to get on track.

The work on the farm was now busier, as there was one less worker to do the tasks. I liked the added responsibility and briefly thought about making it my life's occupation. The weekends were work, bowling, church, and the occasional square dance. I was not, and am not, much of a dancer, but I loved to watch Grandpa and Grandma Stickney dance with their friends. The couples that danced with them became family to me and remained important influences upon me. Just to watch the joy that they all had in dancing, visiting, and sharing of food shaped my view of a simpler life. These couples were farmers, business people, teachers—and all enjoyed their time together. We would gather on Saturday night in an old schoolhouse or grange hall for the evening. Mr. Carlos Howe was the designated square dance caller and was a dear man. He knew his craft and he and his wife Zelda were so much fun. All the ladies would bring potluck dishes, and after a couple of hours of dancing, the food would be brought out and oh my, what a feast there would be. All these people knew hard work and hard times. They enjoyed their time together with dancing and visiting with gusto.

When we weren't dancing, my grandparents and I would go to the new bowling alley that had opened in our little hometown. It was only eight lanes but had two leagues almost every weekday night. Saturday and Sunday were for open bowling. I bowled a lot and became fairly good. I could carry a 180 average and often bowled over 200. I never bowled in leagues, as you had to be eighteen to bowl in a league. I even became interested in the mechanics of the pinsetters and learned how to clear jam ups and other minor problems. There again, it was that cadre of friends of my grandparents who were there to teach and have fun with. The bowling alley had a little snack bar and a jukebox. There were two pinball machines that always attracted my quarters.

A scary event happened when I was sixteen years old. We were putting up a field of hay, which means that we loose stacked the alfalfa for cattle feed. The process was as follows: first you mowed the alfalfa down with a sickle bar mower and let it dry for a couple of days. Then a tractor and a side-delivery rake was used to make windrows. Next the front-end loader with a hay attachment on it picked up the windrows and made a stack in the middle of the field. On this particular day there was a big thunderstorm brewing and my Grandpa Sherm and I were hurrying to get the hay stacked before it got wet with rain. I had just finished the raking and was headed home just as fast as that old John Deere "B" could go. I was on an access road that went to the fields. Beside the road was a pasture, and the pasture had a four-barbwire fence by the road. The fence was lower than the road. A bolt of lightning hit one of the wooden fence post and there was a huge explosion. I remember the explosion but nothing else for a few hours. My Grandma Nellie said that I pulled into the farmyard and stopped the tractor. I got off and was walking towards the house when she met me and asked if Grandpa Sherm was about done stacking the hay. She said that I walked by her and never looked at her or stopped to talk to her. Later, after I told the story of the lightning strike, we went to look at the spot: and all that was left of the wooden fence post was a burned stump. The only reason I was not struck by the lightning, I believe, is that I was on a rubber-tired tractor. I should have been hit by the lightning because I was higher than the post. I had hearing problems for several days, but I fully recovered and still have excellent hearing.

In early 1968, Grandpa Sherm had his first heart attack. It was diagnosed as a mild attack and he was back to work on the farm in no time. By 1971 he had four more heart attacks, each one more damaging than the last. He had a history of heart problems in his family and he suffered from rheumatic fever as a child. One of the side effects of rheumatic fever is a weakening of the heart muscle and heart valves. Add to this the very physical nature of farm work and the mental stress that he had dealt with since 1960, it was a recipe for heart problems. In 1971, Grandpa and Grandma Stickney decided that they would rent out the farm land and just keep and care for the cattle.

Before he rented out the farm land and started the ball rolling for the eventual sale of the farm, he asked my brother and me if we wanted to take over the farm. David said "No," and I also said "No." I was just sixteen years old and not sure where my life journey would be. A part of me really wanted to take it over and to continue Grandpa and Grandma Stickney's legacy. I just could not, though take that step at that time. Several times in the years since, I have kicked myself for turning down the amazing offer.

The result of the five heart attacks make up tragedy number three. My Grandpa Sherm had built the farm into a shining legacy and now he could not continue to do his lifelong love—farming and ranching. God's grace would again show through though. The decision that I made turned out to be the correct one. By me not accepting their offer, they were able to sell the farm, cattle, and machinery and live free of money worries for almost thirty years until their deaths. If I had taken over the farm, Grandpa Sherm would have been there every day to help and advise me. I would, in all likelihood, not have been able to maintain his expectations. It could have caused a family rift and that would have not been good.

CHAPTER 10

HIGH SCHOOL YEARS
AND GOD IS PRESENT

I was now a freshman in a brand-new school. There were fewer students now because the new school only had four grades instead of six. My classroom performance was marginally better, and I did well in the classes that interested me. Vocational agriculture, choir, and speech classes were my favorites. I had matured quite a bit and academics became more important to me. Organized sports were a big draw on my attention and the school district required a certain GPA to play. My grandparents also had their own standards for grades. I rode the school bus every day. I walked one quarter mile from the farmhouse to the gravel road where the bus would pick me up. This walk was done in all kinds of weather. I can only remember a few times that my grandparents would come and give me a ride from the school bus to the farmhouse.

My ending grades for my freshman year were not to the standards of my grandparents and I was not allowed to go out for football my sophomore year at Ravenna High School. I loved football and this decision hurt me deeply. I knew, however, that they were justified in making me accountable for my school work before sports. Instead of rebelling or turning away from family and school, I got the message and worked a little harder to make the grades that I was capable of making. Every year of my schooling, elementary, junior high, and high school, teachers would always comment: "Daniel would be an excellent student if he just applied himself to the school work." Being a very social person, it was hard to give the academics the attention they deserved. I was told by family and teachers that I would regret not learning the school work someday and they were right. I do. Many years later, when I had children of my own, I would say the exact same thing to them. Fortunately, they were much better students than me.

Sophomore year I did much better and I began to meld together the social part of school with academics. My junior year went along smoothly, and I developed a great fondness for speech class and carried that over into a part in the class play. I participated and lettered in three sports: football, wrestling, and track. I purchased my first car from some people we knew. It was a bright red, 1960 Chevrolet Impala two-door coupe. It had a 348 cubic inch motor and a three-speed transmission on the floor. The car originally had a three-speed on the column, but it had gone out. It was beautiful and fast. I then drove myself to school and did not have to ride the school bus. The rules from my grandparents for the car were a lot like the grade rules for sports. Bad grades, no car driving. Any tickets, no car driving. I never lost the use of my car.

Somewhere around October of my junior year, I was in history class listening in on some girls who were talking. As with most small schools, each classmate seemed to have a nickname. Well, there was this girl named Linda—yes, the same Linda as seventh grade-whose nickname was "chicken." When she laughed, she kind of sounded like a chicken cackling. Anyway, she told another girl that no one loved her. I blurted out, "I love you Linda." I have no explanation as to why I said that, but all I know and remember is that it seemed so natural and my heart was in total control. No one called her Linda and Linda and her friends looked at me in amazement. Later in the hall by our lockers, she asked me if I really meant what I had said. I said, "of course I meant it," and I asked if I could call her at home that night. She smiled and said that I could call her. In November, there was a Sadie Hawkins dance scheduled at the school and the tradition was for the girls to ask the boys to the dance. Linda asked me to go and that began a love affair that will last an eternity. At some point that night, we took a walk outside and I asked her if I could kiss her. She said yes and that first kiss was awkward but amazing. Linda lived twelve miles south of town and I had never met her parents. Boy, was I nervous driving out there for that first date. Her parents could not have been nicer, and they still are. The curfew was explained, and we tried to abide by it. I asked Linda to go steady and gave her my class ring around Christmas that year. In the spring we went to the junior prom and the relationship grew slowly.

My senior year was very busy. I again lettered in three sports: football, wrestling, and golf. In football, I played fullback on offense and linebacker on defense. I scored four touchdowns my senior year. In wrestling I won the conference title at the heavyweight class and qualified for districts. At districts, I lost to the eventual state champion. He went on to play professional football for many years. Academics went better than ever, and I participated in many speech competitions. I did "Extemporaneous Speaking," and "TV and Radio Broadcasting." I did a weekly sports report on the school intercom that year. Linda and I were very active in choir and of course we had many dates. Linda was active in the little country Catholic church by their farm, and I was active in the Methodist church in Ravenna. Our individual faith systems seemed to mesh and we did not feel threatened by each other's faith. In the spring we went to our Senior Prom and were voted "Most Unique" in our class. We graduated with fifty-seven other classmates in the spring and I was accepted to attend the University of Nebraska in the fall.

Throughout the summer after graduation, Linda and I talked often about our futures—both together and apart. She got a job at a local factory building parts for pickup campers. On the farm, we still did the haying, but after each cutting was stacked, we went fishing a lot. My grandparents had rented the farm ground out and my Grandpa Sherm, was a fisherman at heart. The relaxation and changing his diet helped his heart condition. They bought a pickup camper and a boat. We went to many of the local reservoirs to fish and I even learned how to waterski. In the fall I went to the university, but Linda and I stayed in nearly constant contact.

CHAPTER 11

HIGHER EDUCATION
OR HAVE A GOOD TIME

When I went to the University of Nebraska, I did not have a major in mind. I took some "General Studies" classes and I thought I would get a revelation as to what I wanted to major in. The result of my noncommittal to a course of study, I believe, caused me to decide that I didn't have to study, and I could just enjoy my freedom in the big city. The University of Nebraska is in Lincoln, Nebraska. Lincoln is the capital of Nebraska and was much larger than my hometown of Ravenna. The University had intermural sports, actual college sports, and all that together meant freedom. There was no one to say, "do this or else." I did not have the personal discipline to make myself study in order to make use of the money that was being spent on this schooling. I regret the wasted time and money. It may have been a blessing because I realized that this coming life would require hard work and that I could not ease through life.

Of all the things I did, some of which I am not proud of, I never dated any girls because of my desire to be faithful to Linda. I traveled home in October to go pheasant hunting. Linda knew that college was not going well for me. Linda and I went on a date and I told her that I would not be going back to the University after the term ended in December. I had bought a diamond ring in Lincoln and on Friday, November 24, I asked Linda Louise Bernadette Miigerl to marry me. God knew that I needed a steadying force in my life and a reason to straighten up and fly right. Linda said "YES!"

The next question was, "What are you/we going to do?" I liked Lincoln and said that I thought we should move to Lincoln and I would get a job. That was okay with her and we made plans to tell the two families the news. We went to her parents first and her dad mentioned that Linda was a Catholic. He never told me I had to convert; he just said, "You know Linda is a Catholic." I said, "Yes Sir, I know that, and I plan to convert." I had been to several Catholic Masses with Linda and I enjoyed the service; it seemed very natural to me. We then went to my grandparents and they gave us their blessings. Grandpa Sherm bristled a little when I said that I was going to convert to Catholicism, but he said, "We all pray to the same God and as long as you remember that, we would be okay." As a little history on our family: my Grandma Stickney was a Catholic before she converted to the Methodist church after marrying my Grandpa Sherm. So, my converting to the Catholic church was like a homecoming.

Linda and her family planned a December 23 wedding. We were married at a small church during a snowstorm. The reception was planned for town fifteen miles from the church. The roads were bad but everyone made it okay and we had a wonderful reception dinner. Shortly after the wedding, we found out we were expecting a baby. We were both excited and felt blessed. The due date was to be July 4. Because my family and I are very patriotic, I thought that the due date had a special significance. It seemed to me that we were being blessed and indeed we were—only the blessing would not arrive on July 4.

CHAPTER 12

STARTING OUR LIFE AS MARRIED FOLK

As a wedding gift to us, Grandpa and Grandma Stickney gave us a 1962 Chevrolet Belair Sedan. The car had very low miles and a little six-cylinder engine with an automatic transmission. We really liked it and the automatic transmission and good gas mileage was good for us newlyweds with a baby on the way. The families and friends were very generous with wedding gifts and we felt blessed to have such a great start to our married life.

We found a very reasonable two-bedroom duplex in Lincoln and two days after we moved I found a job selling Kirby vacuum cleaners. I did that for a month or so, then went to work at Misle Chevrolet in Lincoln as a service runner. The Misle family were very good to me in the short time I worked for them. We traded the 1962 Belair in on a new 1972 Buick Skylark Sun

Coupe. It was a beautiful blue car with a white vinyl sliding sun roof.

In March Grandpa and Grandma Stickney told us that they had sold the farm and they would be having a farm sale and would move into the town of Ravenna. The farm sale was huge, and it took over twelve hours to sell everything. It was painful for all of the family to see all those beautiful registered Hereford cattle being sold. My grandparents, stoic as always, graciously watched their cattle and farm machinery of over forty years of farming being sold to the highest bidder. Grandpa Sherm's brother Wayne, from Oregon, came to the sale. While there, he told me that he was looking for workers for his construction company in La Grande, Oregon. I had been to La Grande twice and was absolutely in love with that city nestled in a beautiful valley surrounded by mountains. The federal government was building Interstate 84 through the outskirts of the city and there were a lot of construction jobs available. Wayne had a house-moving component to his construction company and they were very busy. He said that if I came out to Oregon he would put me right to work. Linda and I talked it over, and we decided that we would move to Oregon for the summer, then see how things were.

On May 3, 1973, we hitched a fully loaded five by seven-foot EZ Haul trailer to the Buick and left for Oregon. None of Linda's family had been to the west coast and they were apprehensive. The coming birth of their first grandchild also raised their level of concern, but I assured them that I would take good care of Linda and the baby.

CHAPTER 13

OREGON: OUR NEW HOME

My great-uncle Wayne and his family lived in La Grande, Oregon. They had a three-generation construction company that specialized in remodeling and house moving. They were a very talented family and did all phases of construction with excellent results.

La Grande is in northeast Oregon. It is the largest city and county seat of Union County, Oregon. La Grande is nestled in the southwest corner of the Grande Ronde Valley. The valley is the largest valley in square miles that is totally surrounded by mountains in the United States. It was settled by several Native American tribes and the first white men were fur traders. When the Oregon Trail settlers came through the valley starting in the 1840s, many of them settled here because of the beauty and the availability of natural resources. The Grande Ronde River winds its way through the valley providing irrigation and recreation. When the Union Pacific Railroad was built in the 1880s, La Grande and the Grande Ronde Valley became a booming area. The valley floor has some of the richest farmland in Oregon. It is surrounded by hundreds of thousands of acres of timber and supports a vibrant timber industry. The cities and towns in the Grande Ronde Valley and Union County are by size: La Grande, Union, Elgin, Imbler, Cove, Island City, North Powder, and Summerville. The Oregon Trail settlers came into the valley from the southeast and skirted along the southern part of the valley and exited at La Grande. The weather in the Grande Ronde Valley definitely has all four seasons.

Two days after arriving in La Grande, Linda and I were taken to watch the annual Collegiate Veterans Raft Race. The race is seven miles down the winding Grande Ronde River to a city park called Riverside Park. It was a real hilarious time of watching fifty to one hundred people floating on rafts and tubes down a very swift and deep river. Add alcohol to the situation and many times calamity ensued. After a few years the race was discontinued due to many factors.

CHAPTER 14

SETTLING INTO A NEW PHASE IN OUR LIVES

Even though we had left the flat plains of Nebraska, and were now in the mountains, the friendliness of the people was amazingly similar. Linda and I, our baby in the womb, and all our possessions arrived on May 5, 1973. We were welcomed by family and they made us feel right at home. We found a little upstairs apartment in downtown La Grande and I started working in construction with my great uncle Wayne and family. Wayne showed us around the city and the Grande Ronde Valley. He introduced us to many of his friends who were also influential people in the community. We were able to find a very good family doctor and we knew that we soon would be needing him to deliver our baby. The Grande Ronde Hospital was very welcoming, and we were confident that our medical needs were in great hands.

We were welcomed at Our Lady of the Valley Catholic Church and that wonderful church family was and continues to be a source of strength for me and my family. Both Linda and I had strong church families in Nebraska and we were overjoyed to find that same Christian love in this brand-new place. We knew absolutely no one in the church but that quickly changed. There seemed to be this amazing mix of older folks and young couples like ourselves. Many of these older ones have gone on, but several of the young couples are still active parishioners, although now we are the older ones.

The construction business was completely new to me, so Wayne and his crew took the time to teach the rookie the ropes. I did not know much about construction, but I was not lazy and wanted to learn all facets of the industry. The house moving part of Wayne's business was the most foreign to me. Getting underneath a fifty-ton house took a little getting used to, but soon I built up a trust in the equipment and my fellow workers who knew that equipment. The heaviest building, we moved was a one hundred and ten-ton two story house. We moved it about a mile with no incidents. When the actual move was taking place, the power company, the phone company, and the cable TV company had to travel along with us to raise the wires so that the moving building could go underneath them. When moving a house, we certainly did not go at break neck speed. Slow, steady, and safe was the motto of house movers. Amazingly, one of the first houses I helped move would later become our family home.

We had moved a month earlier to a ground level duplex. We knew it would easier to have a ground level home with a baby due. On July 11, 1973, a most blessed event occurred. Around one a.m., Linda woke me saying that it was time to go to the hospital. A few hours later, Jason Daniel Pokorney was born. Those days, I could not be in the delivery room, but I was allowed in right after the birth. What a blessing that little boy was and is. After Linda and Jason were resting, I called both families to deliver the great news of the successful birth. I drove to the only restaurant that was open that time of the morning and I could barely eat. Trying to digest the fact that I was now a father, with the responsibilities of that title, was like a ton of bricks on my shoulders. I remember that I prayed out loud for God's help and strength to be a good father. The joy of the moment became a steely resolve to make both families proud and to be the kind of father figure that my Dad and Grandpa had been.

During the months of July and August, we had visits from Grandpa and Grandma Stickney and Linda's dad, mom, and three sisters. All of them doted on the new little guy. Jason was healthy but showed signs of some kind of allergy problem on his skin. He scratched his face a lot and we had to tie little socks on his hands to keep him from injuring himself. After some testing he was diagnosed with eczema. The cause of the eczema was unknown and further testing showed that he was allergic to many foods including chicken eggs and certain nuts.

Once the allergies were under control, Jason was a very active little boy.

CHAPTER 15

BECOMING HOMEOWNERS AND CHANGING JOBS

The move to Oregon in May of 1973 was to be a summer experience. It was now clear to Linda and me that this beautiful city and area would be home for a long time. In early 1974, a house right next to where we were living became available. Actually, it was an old neighborhood grocery store with an attached apartment. The building did not have a foundation, so we could not get a bank loan to remodel the building. We used the inheritance from my parents to buy the house outright. Linda, Jason, and I moved into the living quarters and started the process of digging underneath the entire building so a foundation could be installed. My great uncle Wayne provided technical and physical assistance to get the foundation installed.

Once the foundation was finished, we applied for a home improvement loan to completely remodel the old store side of the building. The newly remodeled space was wonderful for our family. When that was done, we had a wonderful house: a two-bedroom duplex that we lived in and a two-bedroom duplex that we rented out. Having our own home was great and we enjoyed the freedom of decorating like we wanted. Linda was an avid gardener with a definite "green thumb" and a knack for outdoor decorating. She made our property a show place with flowers, vegetable garden, and beautiful lawn. She did all this with very little money. She planted, potted and weeded almost constantly. She would get starts from friends and neighbors and go from there. The soil was very rocky in that part of town so that added to her yard work. Many loads of topsoil had to be purchased to make the garden a workable area. Being landlords was not a good experience. We found out that we were too easy going and many renters moved out owing money, and some had damaged the apartment.

About the same time as the home purchase took place, the construction work declined to the point that I needed to find a different job. I found a job in farming with the Bingaman family. Howard and Arla Bingaman were wonderful people and reminded me of my own family in the way that they operated their farm. I soon found out that farming in northeastern Oregon is much different than Nebraska. For one thing they grew wheat. On our farm in Nebraska we could not grow wheat because of the sandy soil. The fields were much larger in acreage in Oregon and some of the fields were on very hilly ground. On the hilly ground they used track-type tractors for the traction needed to pull the machinery that was much wider than we had used in Nebraska.

The Bingaman's farming operation is truly an historic family business. At least four generations of the Bingaman family have farmed and ranched in the Grande Ronde Valley of northeastern Oregon. They practice sound farming principles and add to the economic base of Union County with a wide variety of crops. There is the love of the land and the love of the animals, just as in Nebraska where I grew up. I had the chance to meet many families in the Grande Ronde Valley that came from pioneer stock. It was a joy to build friendships with those folks and those friendships remain to this day with those who are left and their families. I honor the memory of Howard and Arla Bingaman and treasure the friendship that I share with their family members.

I worked for two spring, summer, and fall seasons for the Bingaman family and was unemployed during the winter months. Those months were hard times. I had to apply for food stamps in order for the family to make it through the winter. When using the food stamps, we would go shopping late at night because we viewed the use of food stamps as shameful. I also received just $63 per week unemployment pay from the State of Oregon. That humbling time left an indelible mark on our little family. I took pride in working to support the family and did all I could to always have a job. We were fortunate that assistance programs like that was available for those truly in need. When I went to work for the Bingaman family, I bought a nice 1963 Ford half-ton pickup to commute to the farm each day. It was a great truck and as with all my cars and trucks, I wish I could and would have kept them all. We of course were very active at the church and those friendships would very soon become a catalyst for another big change for our young family. Even though the hard times were not tragic, they were difficult and the chance to give up was there. God saw to this and gave grace to this young family in the form of a caring friend who went out of his way to help with the possibility of full-time employment.

CHAPTER 16

BOISE CASCADE—A CHANCE FOR LONG-TERM EMPLOYMENT

In March of 1976, I was working outside in my garage when a friend of mine, that I knew from church called me on the phone. His job was in Human Resources at a company called Boise Cascade, a timber and wood products company with nationwide operations. In 1976 they were the largest employer in Union County. The wood products industry was something I knew nothing about but I knew they paid a good wage. When my friend called and asked me if I could come down for an interview on a possible job, I said "Yes." When I got to his office, we walked out to an area of the sawmill where there were several men pulling newly sawed boards off of a moving chain that was about waist high. The men were also stacking boards by size and length. My friend and I met the foreman of the workers and he asked me if I thought I could do that job. I was a young, muscular, and confident man and I said, "You mean all I have to do is pull those boards off the moving chain and stack them?" He said that the boards, at times, came by very fast and all sizes were mixed up. After a little more conversation, the foreman told my friend that he would take a chance on me.

My friend and I went back to his office to complete paperwork for my new job. He mentioned that there was a backlog of applicants and that he had skipped several of them in order to give me a chance. I thanked him and told him he would not be sorry. God gave my friend the strength to make a decision that could possibly get him in trouble and God gave me the strength to give this new opportunity my best effort. He said that this was a full-time union job, and much was expected of me. As I was leaving, feeling on top of the world, he asked me if I wanted to know what the pay would be. I remember saying, "Oh anything is fine." When he told me that the wage was $5.80 per hour, I said, "You mean every hour?"

I went home to Linda and Jason and we were all happy as could be. I remember doing some rough calculations of the wages and said that we would have more money than we would know what to do with. Of course, that was not the case totally. Life did become, at least financially, easier than it had been. We gave more time and treasure to the church and to community groups. Linda and I taught an eighth- grade church class and I started lectoring (proclaiming the Mass readings) at Mass.

The work at the Boise Cascade Sawmill was far from easy. It was physically demanding work and we were outside in all kinds of weather. I had to dress for the weather conditions, but I also had to have movement capabilities in order to do the job right. The green cut lumber came out of the sawmill on a series of running flat chains. The lumber was all thicknesses, lengths, and widths. The boards were sorted by the workers according to the dimensions. This process was called the 'green chain' because the boards were moving on a chain and they were fresh-cut from logs. The boards would be called 'green' until they were later dried, planed smooth, and shipped world-wide as lumber. In addition to the difficulty of the work and weather, I had to learn to get along with a wide variety of personalities I worked with. The timber and wood products industry drew a hardened worker and they were often very hard-living folk. I had never been around people with such different lifestyles and I was viewed as an outsider in the interactions with fellow workers. I was, for instance, the only worker on the 'green chain' who was still married to his first wife. All that being said, I did make some friends on the job and learned that each individual has his own lot in life.

CHAPTER 17

GROWING UP TOGETHER
AS A FAMILY

Jason started pre-school classes at a private pre-school/ kindergarten school. At that time the La Grande School District did not offer kindergarten classes. He flourished with excellent teachers at the pre-school and we contributed to the learning with family time working with numbers, reading, and writing. Jason was an enthusiastic learner and looked forward to 'regular' school. I remember that on his first day of pre-school, I asked him what he had learned, and he said, "Girls go first." It is never too early to learn good manners.

Jason started regular school at a neighborhood elementary school just three blocks from our house. The school was called Riveria and was a two-story brick building that eerily resembled the country school I had attended in Poole, Nebraska. A full-size gymnasium was attached to Riveria School and within that gymnasium was the cafeteria, and an all-purpose room. Riveria housed grades one through six. It was a full service elementary school with a principal, wonderful teachers, library, music, and resource room. There was also a very active parent group called The Riveria Partners. Linda and I became active with the Partners and remained in leadership roles for the six years that Jason attended. The Riveria Partners worked in close association with the great staff and supported many wonderful school events. One such event was a Halloween carnival that is still going on in the building even though the building is no longer a school. The school still stands and is a community center with a variety of community programs. The carnival is called Spook-a-Rama. For over forty years, this fun family event has happened in that little neighborhood and the entire community strongly supports it.

My first taste of getting involved in the community was through the principal's office at Riveria. On one side of the school, staff and visitors could park their vehicles in a parking area off the street. It was a gravel street and when there was a big rain or when the snow was melting, a lake would form which made parking difficult. I met with the principal and asked if something could be done to help the water-hole situation. He told me that giving my comments to the superintendent would have more of an impact than if he (as the principal) was asking. Linda and I then met with the superintendent and he asked if we would address the school board on the issue (at the school board meeting). We did, and we received some help in the form of a load of gravel which helped a lot. Little did I know then that this event would lead to a career in volunteer service to our beloved La Grande, Oregon.

Ravenna, Nebraska, Thursday, July 28, 1960

Elaborate Floral Display at Multiple Funeral

Multiple funeral services were held Saturday at the high school for the four members of the Wm. Pokorney family killed last week in an auto collision in Wyoming. The entire stage of the high school auditorium was banked with flowers. Over 700 persons attended the funeral service. Rev. Jacobson of the Methodist church officiated. There were 22 pallbearers, and four hearses were used. Burial was in Highland Park cemetery, Ravenna. It is the first time in Ravenna history that a funeral for this number or with this attendance, was held.

Picture of the funeral held for William Sr. Ruby Jeanne, Thomas, and William Jr. The auto accident was July 18, 1960. Funeral was July 23, 1960. The funeral was held in the Ravenna High School Auditorium to accommodate the large number of mourners.

Leaving on the ill-fated vacation July 16, 1960
L to R: Sophia Pokorney, William Pokorney Jr., Thomas Pokorney,
Nellie Stickney, Sherman Stickney, Daniel Pokorney,
William Pokorney Sr., David Pokorney

July 18 - 1960 =

The four brothers together for the last time.

Ten hours later we were separated by a deadly car accident.

L to R: Daniel age 6, Thomas age 9, William Jr. age 4, David age 10

William and Ruby Jeanne (Stickney) Pokorney

My father and mother's Wedding. 1948

Sherman and Nellie Stickney 50th Wedding Anniversary. 1978.

L to R: David Pokorney, Daniel Pokorney,

Sherman Stickney, Nellie Stickney

Daniel and Linda (Miigerl) Pokorney Wedding. 1972

Linda Pokorney (my wife) tending her fabulous flowers. 1994

Home on leave from the U.S. Navy. 1994

L to R: DaLyn Pokorney, Jason Pokorney, Diedra Pokorney

Good mess of fish caught at Anthony Lakes, Oregon. 1990

L to R: Daniel Pokorney, Jason Pokorney, Sherman Stickney

Daniel and Linda Pokorney and children. 1991
L to R: Diedra Pokorney, Jason Pokorney, Linda Pokorney,
Daniel Pokorney, DaLyn Pokorney

Daniel and Linda Pokorney 25th Wedding Anniversary. 1997

L to R: Daniel, DaLyn, Linda, Jason, Marci, and Diedra Pokorney

Daniel Pokorney taking the oath of office as the
Mayor of La Grande, Oregon. 2011

Destry and DaLyn Anderson. Coeur d' Alene, Idaho. 2013

L to R: Marci, Jason, and Delaney Pokorney. 2018

A marker erected at the Pokorney Memorial Tree
at the residence of Daniel Pokorney. 2018

CHAPTER 18

OUR YOUNG FAMILY FACES HARD TIMES

In the fall of 1979, our family learned that we were expecting another child. The anticipation was high, and we planned for an addition to the home to make room for another blessing. Very early in the pregnancy, something went wrong or something was not right with the baby and we suffered a miscarriage. We were all devastated, but Linda was especially hit hard. We prayed for strength and understanding, from God. Our church friends and both of our families were also trying to help us cope with the loss. No matter what we tried, Linda's depression deepened to a level that I had never seen. From the time as school classmates, when we got to know one another, Linda would have times of depression that seemed more than just being down for a day or so. She used to call those her 'moody' times. About six months after the miscarriage, we went to a local psychologist who diagnosed Linda with post-partum depression. He prescribed some medication that only masked the real problem. In 1982 we went to another doctor who, when looking at family history and Linda's mood swings, diagnosed manic depression. Today manic depression is known as bi-polar disorder. With that diagnosis came treatment options that helped Linda immediately, although not completely, but at least we knew what illness we were dealing with. Linda would battle the effects of bi-polar disorder for the rest of her life—until a more evil and unforgiving illness would take its place in her and our lives. The miscarriage would be the fourth tragedy in my life and the grace that followed it was a certain amount of peace-of-mind regarding Linda's health. The grace also re-affirmed our belief that God was in charge and if He wasn't ready for us to have another child, then we were to go on with our lives.

We went through with the building of a 24'x24' addition onto the house. The larger space was great and it seemed to give Linda a positive outlook. We now had a three-bedroom, two-bath duplex with a much larger living room area. We also rearranged the outside of the house and the yard. Linda had taken the Master Gardener class from the Oregon State University Extension Service. She was certified, and she gladly put her expertise into practice with the new yard and lot design. She truly had a 'green thumb' and enjoyed the beauty that her hard work produced.

Even with the stresses at home, Jason did well in school and was helped along by Linda and me, a caring school staff, and a loving church family. The tragic loss of a child was not only difficult for Linda, but Jason and I suffered also. I cannot speak for Jason, but I know I felt an emptiness and an inadequacy as a father. I could not, however, let that feeling affect my family or work responsibilities. I just put my nose to the grindstone and forged ahead. In retrospect, I believe that counseling could have helped our family.

I was still working a swing shift (5 p.m. to 1:30 a.m.) at the Boise Cascade Sawmill. I had moved from the "green chain" to operating a machine called the "Dropout," an operation where I judged every board that was cut in the sawmill. Any board that needed to be re-sawed to either clean-up the side of the board or trim the end to the correct length, had to be returned inside the sawmill for correction. The job was very stressful, and the boards would often come in front of me three, four, and five boards deep. If the board was okay, I sent it down a long chain where it would be graded by a fellow worker and sorted automatically. If the board needed to be re-sawed, I opened a hydraulic gate and the board would drop onto a set of rollers, then go back into the sawmill where it would be corrected. I had to stand the entire shift and operated three toggle switches and an up and down handle for the hydraulic gate. I also had two foot switches that ran a different set of chains. Behind me was a switch panel with about twenty switches for still more sets of chains and rollers. If there was ever a time when there were no boards coming to me, I had a lot of clean-up to do. The job was very challenging and since there was no one there to help me with the process, I learned to accept this responsibility of watching every board that was cut in the sawmill. This building up of my confidence would be a great asset to me in my future.

The wood products industry is a very cyclical industry. One moment you are booming and the next you are dealing with the threat of layoff. In 1984, a terrible economy and rising costs forced Boise Cascade to shut down the swing shift at the La Grande Sawmill and Planer. All of the hourly workers at the sawmill and planer were union workers and the layoff went by seniority. I did not have enough seniority to hold a job there, so I went into layoff status. The unemployment insurance pay was barely adequate to sustain the family, and it did not keep up the standard of living that we were accustomed to. There was a chance of recall to the sawmill for up to two years, but I chose not to sit around and wait. I wanted to be a solid provider for our family and drawing "rocking chair," was not the way to do it.

I chose to enroll at Eastern Oregon State College in La Grande and take some courses in preparation of potential job change. I was accepted to EOSC and took a class load of 15 credit hours. I was much more mature in 1984 than I was in 1972 when I had unsuccessfully tried college level work. I did well at college. Because I was very interested in the education field, I filed to run for election to a position on the Union Education Service District Board of Directors. I was not successful at my first attempt at running for public office, but I had a desire to serve the community in a positive way. I really felt that I, as a blue-collar worker, had a perspective on governance that was not being heard from in the community.

CHAPTER 19

A BIG CHANCE AND
SOME BIG DECISIONS

While I was still taking classes at EOSC, Boise Cascade called in February of 1985 and asked if I wanted to transfer to an entry level position at the Boise Cascade Particleboard Plant which was just five miles outside of La Grande. I agreed and was told that I would be on the graveyard shift 11:30 p.m. to 7:30 a.m. I was taking a chance on whether I would like the job and fellow workers and if I could endure the overnight work hours. I planned to finish the term I was enrolled in at the college and continue working: college during the day and work at night. Well, it got real hard to juggle college, work, and family. I seemed to acclimate well to the particleboard plant, which was completely different work from the sawmill. I did not enroll at the college after the spring term.

Jason was ending his elementary school studies and would move to the Middle School in the fall of 1985. Linda and I discussed the fact that we were relatively young and maybe we should give parenthood another try. Linda's illness seemed to be much more stable, and we were assured by the doctors that the medication she was taking was safe for a possible pregnancy. We learned in April of 1985 that we were expecting a baby. The due date was December 21 and the preparations started.

I was adjusting to the graveyard shift work hours and Linda spent her days planning and preparing for a new little one. Linda always was very cognizant of my need to sleep during the day. She always kept the noise to a minimum and was always concerned for me. I usually slept from 8:30 a.m. to around 2 p.m. I then would try and get a nap in from 8:00 p.m. to 10:00 p.m. It seems odd but that is the life of the shift worker. I have a profound respect for the people in our lives that do the needed shift work. Police, fire, and nurses are just some of the dedicated people who sacrifice and work the overnight hours to serve us all.

Around June, with the pregnancy going well, Linda's doctor was concerned at how big she was getting this early in the pregnancy. Dr. Thomas Geraci was a family friend and fellow parishioner at church and he suggested an ultrasound so that any possible problems could be addressed. There was a medical reason for the concern about the early large size, but I do not recall what that is called. Linda and I agreed with the stipulation that we not be told the sex of the baby. We were old-fashioned in that regard. We did not know the sex of our babies before they arrived. The day arrived, and we went to the hospital for the ultrasound. I got to be in the room and was watching the monitor along with Linda and the specialist doing the ultrasound. He located a baby and quickly moved to another part of her abdomen so that we would not see the sex of the baby. He moved towards the top of her abdomen and said, "There is another baby." Linda and I looked at each other with mouths agape and eyes wide open. He continued to move the machine around on her abdomen and Linda finally said, "Will you stop looking? I am not going to have a litter."

We went home and tried to let it soak in that we were going to have twins. There actually were several sets of twins in both our families; however, they were two and three generations back. When we told our families and friends, they were all excited. Linda's planning now had changed: we needed double everything. The twin's room was going to be Jason's old room and he was going to move to our old bedroom. Jason's room was painted a light blue and Linda said, "There is no sense painting this room because these twins are going to be boys." She was convinced. She had me convinced. It seemed like all the indications were telling her that they were boys. We were so convinced that the babies were boys, that we had only boys' names in mind.

I had decided to run for a position on the La Grande School Board of Directors. The election would be in the spring of

1986. I had gone to several school board meetings and I really thought I could provide a voice from not only the blue-collar worker point of view, but also the north side of La Grande point of view. One of the problems in running for this particular office was that the meetings almost always ran late into the night and since I was working the graveyard shift, I would have to leave the meetings before they were over. Should I be elected, I had a plan that would alleviate this problem. I had tremendous support from all of the PTAs at the five elementary schools, because of my work and association with them during my time working with the Riveria Partners.

CHAPTER 20

READY OR NOT, HERE WE COME

Jason started seventh grade in the fall at the beautiful and spacious La Grande Middle School. The school housed all the seventh and eighth grade students from the entire district. The school had a wonderful staff and Jason did well there.

Linda was increasingly uncomfortable, as can be expected, but we were still planning on a birth somewhere around Christmas. Dr. Geraci had arranged for another doctor to assist him with the delivery when it came time. Linda's birthday was on November 21 and she was miserable. Thanksgiving was coming up on November 28 and I told her I would handle the cooking duties. Very early on November 28, Linda woke me saying that it was time to go to the hospital. This was a month early, but we needed to go—NOW. When we got to the hospital the nursing staff called the doctors and said that Linda was in full labor. Before we went into the delivery room, the doctors told us of their concern. Sometimes babies delivered, a month early, might not have their lungs fully developed. This fact, plus the fact that they were twins, only heightened the doctors concern. They did a test of the amniotic fluid and it seemed to suggest that all would be well to let the labor continue. They did advise us that if the babies had breathing problems, they might have to be transferred to Portland, Oregon, to the neo-natal center there.

I got to be with Linda in the delivery room this time. There were two trusted doctors, a team of nurses, and a very nervous mom and dad in that room. Oh yeah, there were two little babies just waiting to make their grand entrance too. On November 28, Thanksgiving Day 1985, Linda gave birth to two beautiful baby girls. That's right—girls. You can imagine mom and dad's surprise when each one of the girls made her appearance. DaLyn Elizabeth was born first at 5lbs 4oz followed by Diedra Marie at 5lbs 1oz. What a special Thanksgiving Day that was for us. To this day, Dr. Thomas Geraci remembers that day and we always mention it when we meet. DaLyn was doing well, but Diedra was breach and there was concern for her. Both girls were put on special machines and monitored constantly.

We waited about an hour before we gave the baby girls their names because we had not really discussed possible girl names. Linda was amazing during the birth and was able to discuss the names before she went to sleep. We liked DaLyn because it was a combining of mine and Linda's first names. She wanted the "Y" just to make the name look snappier and she wanted the name to be two distinct syllables with the emphasis on the second syllable. She liked Diedra because she heard it on a television show. The middle names were given because they just sounded like they went with the first names. Both little girls were a little jaundiced but were breathing on their own. That meant that their lungs were developed enough for them to be able to stay at the hospital where they were born. After Linda went to sleep and the girls were settled, I went home to tell Jason about his new sisters. He was as surprised as we were. I took a nap, then Jason and I went to the hospital and had a hospital Thanksgiving dinner with Linda. Jason saw his sisters for the first time and said, "They sure are small." The twins were "fraternal" and did not really look alike. DaLyn resembled me and Diedra really looked like Linda. DaLyn and Diedra spent 5 days in the hospital before they came home to mom, dad, and big brother.

Jason was twelve years old, and he was so responsible that it was like having another adult to help. We knew that we were having twins since July and thought that we had prepared ourselves for coming home with two little ones. Nope. It was a whole different world. They were good babies, but everything happened twice and sometimes at the same time. The girls became aware of each other fairly quickly and seemed to want to be together. As I said earlier, Linda did a great job of keeping them as quiet as possible because I needed to sleep during the day. Fortunately, their room was at the other end of the house, so she spent most of her time with the girls in their room. Jason was a big help at night when I was working. How lucky we were to have such a great big brother to help.

CHAPTER 21

THE VOTERS SAY YES AND ANOTHER SETBACK FOR THE FAMILY

The election for the La Grande School Board of Directors was held in the spring of 1986 and I was elected to a four-year term. One of the first items I addressed on the school board was the length of the meetings. The monthly meetings routinely lasted from 7:30 p.m. until often past 1:00 a.m. Since I was still working the graveyard shift, I suggested that we have a monthly work session and then a regular monthly meeting. That would mean an extra meeting each month, but there would not be any more late-night meetings. The proposal took an a while to get passed. I urged my fellow board members and the superintendent to at least try the new schedule. The new schedule was popular with the administrators. They disliked the late-night meetings because they had a short night and then back to the schools in the morning. After about a year, the school board adopted the new meeting schedule.

The national economy was in a recession in the mid-1980s and our family was hit hard. Boise Cascade Corporation, the company I was working for, was also hit hard by the recession. They imposed a wage and benefit cut to all employees. The premise of the wage cut was to make the company more competitive in the wood products industry. The result of the wage cut reduced my paychecks to the point that we could not make mortgage payments. (We had the original mortgage on the house and a second mortgage to remodel and add-on before the birth of the twins.) We tried the "Rob Peter to pay Paul" technique for several months but it only resulted in getting further behind. The stress was evident on the family and the last thing Linda needed was more stress. We looked into trying to sell the house, but the entire area was in a very depressed financial situation. The only way out was to do a "Deed in Lieu of Foreclosure." That meant walking away from all that we had done to our home both inside and out.

This would become the fifth tragedy for me and I was seriously doubting my ability to deal with this severe financial setback. The grace of God became clear very quickly as my grandparents owned a home in La Grande. It was the very house that I had helped move there in 1974 and they were using it as rental property. They told us to move into the home. I immediately started cleaning up the house and doing a fair amount of remodeling. The second story was a storage area and I finished off a 150 square foot area for a bedroom. Jason would occupy the upstairs room and the twins would share a room on the main floor. Linda and I had a bedroom on the main floor also. The kitchen was large and there was a large dining/living room area. It had a big front porch that was the full-width of the house. The house set back from the street and there was a nice-sized front yard. Right after the twins celebrated their first birthday, the family moved into a house made possible by generous grandparents and the grace of God.

CHAPTER 22

LIFE SETTLES DOWN BUT REMAINS BUSY

Jason loved football and I helped coach him in seventh grade football which was sponsored by the Optimist Club. In eighth grade, football was a school sponsored sport through the middle school. He did well and played the center position. He liked being a vital part of each play. We practiced a lot at home on long snaps to the punter. His time at the La Grande Middle School continued to be positive and he did well in his studies as well as sports and choir. Jason auditioned for a role in an Eastern Oregon State College production of "Macbeth" and played the role of one of Macbeth's sons. He later performed in a production of "West Side Story" at the college. He played Baby John, one of the Jets gang. He really enjoyed the singing, dancing and acting.

DaLyn and Diedra were happy girls and Linda had them outside whenever possible. We lived just two blocks from a city park which they enjoyed. We had great next-door neighbors on each side of us. They both were retired couples who became like proxy grandparents to the girls. Linda's parents and family came to Oregon when they could, and we traveled to Nebraska many, many times. My grandparents visited once a year, and even though they were Grandpa and Grandma to the twins, they were, in fact, Great Grandpa and Grandma to them. Our families lived thirteen hundred miles from us but they were always there when we needed them.

On one such visit to Nebraska I wanted to take the twins to the hometown golf course. I rented a power cart and the three of us were having a good time. I played and the girls enjoyed riding along and holding the flag on the greens for me. On the second to the last hole, the green is on the top of a hill. As I was putting, Diedra stayed at the cart while DaLyn and I went over to the green. Diedra was sitting in the cart and I told her not to touch any of the controls. Well, she somehow released the brake and the cart started to roll down the hill. Diedra yelled at me and we started to chase the cart. The cart was a three wheeled cart with a canopy. She jumped out of the cart and grabbed the canopy post on the front of the driver's side and the cart turned quickly towards her. The cart went completely over her and then I was there to stop it. Deidra was laying on the grass and her leg was bent at an odd angle. It looked bad and the first thing I thought of was that Linda was going to kill me for getting Deidra hurt. I slowly helped her to her feet and amazingly she was basically unhurt. The ground was soft and I think that saved her from serious injury. That heavy cart had gone over her but instead of a terrible injury, the family had another story to tell and relive for the ages.

Linda always had a fantastic vegetable garden and flowers were everywhere. DaLyn and Diedra were the designated "helpers" for mom outside and inside. I was still working the graveyard shift and I was blessed that most days I had peace and quiet for my sleeping time. I continued with my service on the La Grande School Board, and even though the issues were difficult, I certainly felt that I was making a difference for the better. In 1990 I ran for re-election to the School Board and won. I was also honored to be selected by my fellow board members to serve as the school board chairman for two consecutive years, 1993 and 1994. I served eight years, then voluntarily did not seek re-election. During my school board service, I was lucky enough to get to know many wonderful people in education. I was relatively young when I was elected to the school board and there were many seasoned board members who helped me learn budgeting and other important items. My family always supported my public service and that helped me tremendously. The impact of money on the education of students needs to be balanced and the need for dollars from the community cannot exceed the ability of the community to pay.

Our church family remained strong with Jason serving as an altar server and I was serving as a Lector. When the twins were eight years old, they would follow big brother's service to the church by being altar servers also. Diedra and DaLyn served as altar servers for ten years until they graduated from high school. All three children were very involved in religious education classes and the fine instruction they received from various teachers helped them to develop in their faith. I myself became an Installed Acolyte in 2005 and served at the Our Lady of the Valley Parish. I assisted the priests at the altar. I also led many rosary services, adorations, and for eight years I led the Stations of the Cross services each Friday of the Lenten season. I was an Installed Acolyte for ten years before resigning in 2015. My resignation came about because I had made a volunteer position into a job. Yes, I was at the altar and yes it was wonderful being that close to the beautiful Catholic Mass. I however, was many times concentrating on the next task I would be doing at the Mass, instead of concentrating on the scripture and homily. Since leaving my service at the altar, I have a renewed appreciation for the Mass and can now concentrate on the important words of God.

Jason entered La Grande High School in the fall of 1987 and was very busy with academics, sports, acting, and choir. Jason had a very successful high school career. He had roles in musicals and plays and was member of the La Grande High School Acapella and Select Choirs. The choirs performed locally and at state contests. I was honored to accompany the La Grande Choirs on a performance tour of San Francisco. All members, and the choir director J. Michael Frasier were well received wherever they performed. Jason also excelled on the football field for the La Grande High School Tigers. He played the center position on the offensive line. He was selected as All Conference Honorable Mention his Senior year 1990/91.

Jason always had the goal to serve in the United States Navy aboard an aircraft carrier. He went through the military testing and did an early enlistment. All papers were signed and we all knew his reporting date to basic training. His report date was after his high school graduation in July of 1991. His basic training was at Great Lakes Naval Training Station in Chicago, Illinois. Linda was able to go to his graduation from basic training and enjoyed the pageantry and reverence of the ceremony. Jason's next training was "A" school" in Virginia Beach, Virginia. While at "A" school" he received his training for his upcoming job with the Navy. He qualified as a Radar Operations Specialist. It was also at this time that he was assigned the ship he would serve on. Like I said, he wanted an aircraft carrier and he was fortunate to be assigned to the *USS Carl Vinson-CV 70*. The *Carl Vinson* is a Nimitz Class nuclear aircraft carrier with a crew of around six thousand sailors, pilots, and a contingent of United States Marines.

CHAPTER 23

ONE GRADUATED AND TWO JUST STARTING SCHOOL

Diedra and DaLyn started kindergarten in 1991, the year Jason graduated from high school. They attended Willow Elementary School just four blocks from our house. Between our house and school however, was a major state highway and the Union Pacific Railroad tracks. The girls were feeling very independent and I believe that the they walked to school together alone for the first time in the spring of second grade. Willow School was another one of the great neighborhood elementary schools in La Grande. It was a brick building that housed one class each of K-6 grades. The staff was excellent, and the girls did well in school. In third grade however, Diedra began to struggle so they tested her for attention deficit disorder (ADD). Diedra would struggle at times, like taking tests, but managed the ADD all through her schooling. She worked hard to compensate and we as a family helped also. In true Diedra style, she would eventually overcome a lot of the problems with ADD. ADD people are most often creative people and Diedra was no exception. DaLyn and Diedra went through elementary school with many good friends and especially loved and respected the teachers and school staff. In sixth-grade, DaLyn was honored by being elected the class president. That meant she was the sixth-grade representative to the student council.

DaLyn and Diedra also started dancing with the Becky Thompson School of Dance in La Grande. The dance school had students from age six to high school and beyond. The dance school offered tap, ballet, jazz, and interpretive dance instruction. The girls loved to dance and perform in the community. They stayed with the dance school all the way into their high school years.

Linda's love of her flowers and everything outside deepened even more during the time the girls attended school. She began to start tomatoes from seed and raised them to plants about twelve inches high. She then sold some of them to friends, but she gave many away so that other folks might have the opportunity to grow their own produce. We had a yard sale once, and she gave away thirty to forty tomato plants to anyone who wanted them.

I was still working the graveyard shift at Boise Cascade and for several years the industry was stable. I was serving my second term as a member of the La Grande School Board and so enjoyed working with the school district staff, my fellow board members, parents, and students. We wanted to make the La Grande School District the best it could be. Education is so important, especially at the local level.

Jason was serving in the United States Navy aboard the *USS Carl Vinson*. The *Carl Vinson* and its battle group left in 1994 for a six-month deployment on a western Pacific tour (WestPac) and the Persian Gulf region. They visited several ports-of-call but the main reason for the deployment was to patrol and be a stabilizing presence in a war torn and volatile area of the world. It was a stressful time for the family because Jason was in harms way. We had to rely on our faith in God that with his training and the leadership of the military he would be kept safe and the world would be safe from despots. Upon Jason's safe return we had a brief celebration of thanksgiving to God for our loved one's safety. It is so amazing and wonderful that young men and women choose to serve in the military. Their sense of purpose and resolve is comforting to those of us whom they are protecting all day—every day.

CHAPTER 24

WE WELCOME A NEW
FAMILY MEMBER

While Jason was at sea, a wedding was being planned. Jason Pokorney and Marci Lester had met at La Grande High School and dated for two years prior to Jason's graduation. Jason went into the Navy and Marci attended the University of Oregon, but they remained friends. Ten days after Jason returned from the naval deployment, on August 27, 1994, Jason Daniel Pokorney and Marci Ann Lester were wed at the First Baptist Church in La Grande, Oregon. Jason was attended by three shipmates from the *USS Carl Vinson* and Marci was attended by long time friends and classmates. Diedra and DaLyn were junior brides-maids. Linda and I hosted a rehearsal dinner at the La Grande Country Club and all the flowers came from Linda's extensive garden. Marci's parents, Lonnie and Ruth Lester, hosted the wedding reception and one of the main decorations was peacock feathers from their farm. The wedding was a beautiful day with many friends, relatives, and community members attending. God blessed the union and all of us attending.

Marci is the youngest of the four daughters of Lonnie and Ruth (Hoxie) Lester. Both the Lester and the Hoxie families are multi-generational families in the Grande Ronde Valley and La Grande area. The Lesters are a strong family in business and strong in their faith in God.

After the wedding, Jason and Marci moved to Concord, California where Jason was stationed aboard the aircraft carrier. Jason re-enlisted in the Navy for four more years in 1994.

CHAPTER 25

OUR WORLD IS TURNED UPSIDE DOWN

In the spring of 1994, Linda was preparing another great garden and flower beds all around the yard. One day, when I woke up from my day sleep, she told me that she was having trouble weeding the flowers by hand because she could not grasp the weed and pull it out of the ground. She said it was like she had no strength in her hand. There was no pain, just no strength. This went on for a couple of weeks, so I suggested she go to the chiropractor who was a friend of ours. I was thinking she had a pinched nerve or something like that. After x rays showed no problems, she was sent to an orthopedic doctor for further diagnosis. The orthopedic doctor could find nothing and suggested a neurologist. The grip problem started in Linda's right hand, but now it was affecting her right hand and arm and now the left hand. She was having trouble signing her name and other small tasks that we all do with our hands. Linda was always very good at arts and crafts, but now she had a hard time doing any of that. We went to the neurologist in Walla Walla, Washington, and he started tests. At first it was physical testing such as walking, arm movements, and resistance to pressure. She was given CAT scans, MRIs, and other tests in order to get a diagnosis. All this testing took several months to complete and when he could not determine the cause of the ailment, he suggested extensive blood tests that would be sent to a hospital specializing in neuro-muscular testing. When all the tests were back, and no definite cause found, the neurologist made an appointment with a specialist at the Oregon State Health Science University Hospital in Portland, Oregon.

On February 28, 1995 we met Dr. Wendy Johnson at OHSU. She reviewed the testing and did a small amount of strength testing herself. When she was finished, she came into the room and gave us the diagnosis: amyotrophic lateral sclerosis (ALS). I guess we looked at her with puzzled expressions, so she said the disease is commonly known as Lou Gehrig's Disease. I looked at Linda and I could see that she still did not know what it was. I turned to the doctor and said, "Isn't that always fatal?" Many times, I have been sorry for the way in which I blurted out that comment, but it was the first thing that came to my mind. I was shocked by the words that the doctor spoke and was hoping that maybe the end result could be different in Linda's case. The doctor sadly said "Yes." She said it was true that Lou Gehrig's Disease is always fatal. Linda was in shock and said, "Wait! What? Are you sure?" The doctor said that she was very sure of the diagnosis because all of the bases had been covered and that neuro-muscular disease was her specialty. She said that Linda would have two to five years to live. The disease would be progressive and it would eventually affect the muscles you need the most—the internal organs. She explained that amyotrophic lateral sclerosis, or ALS, stops the nerves from being able to stimulate and engage the muscles. Because the muscles are not moving, they atrophy and become ineffective. She said that ALS was a good news/bad news disease. The good news was that because the muscles are not being used and are shrinking away, there would not be any pain. The bad news was that your mind would not be affected, and that you would know and see what was happening to you and there was nothing you could do about it.

She told us that she believed that this form of ALS was sporadic, meaning that it was not hereditary from any ancestors or to our children. ALS affects about five thousand new people worldwide each year, and it usually affects men more than women. Linda was forty one years old when she was diagnosed, which is usually in the range of when ALS is diagnosed.

The doctor said that we would be contacted if any new treatment or cure for ALS was found. On that date and to the present, the cause of ALS is not known. Therefore, a treatment or cure is not available. Patients who live longer than five years usually have to be on some sort of artificial life support in order to breath. She suggested that we contact a support group in order to help us deal with this terrible disease. I thought to myself, "I do not need a support group." My wife was just given a death sentence. We need God to help us through this. We were devastated.

The 260-mile drive back to La Grande was solemn. DaLyn and Diedra were with us and they sat quietly in the backseat as Linda and I discussed what to do, how to do it, cried, and questioned the meaning of this huge and permanent crisis in our lives. Linda remarked that we needed to tell the family first. Also, she said that we should have all our ducks in a row when we talked to family. We would try to answer the questions that we knew would be asked, if we knew the answers. Next, we would talk to our priest, Father Hank Albrecht, to help us understand what our faith's teaching and guidelines are as to how we should prepare and handle issues with Linda's care. After that we would tell selected friends in our church family, the school staff so they could support the girls if they were having a bad day, community members, and my employer. We knew the word would get out, and we were not averse to that, except that we did not want pity, only prayerful support.

Informing the family was very difficult, but Linda was a rock when delivering the word. We could not answer questions like, "How did you get this?" or "Isn't there a medicine or something to help?" Everyone was very supportive and said that each of them would do all they could to help. At that time, we just asked them to pray that God's will be done and each of us would find peace of mind to accept this path that God had chosen for Linda. The school staff, my employer, and the community were ready to help in any way they could. In our visit with Father Hank, he told us the church required only two things in terminal illness cases: Pain should be controlled as best that it can be, and that the person should be sufficiently hydrated. Any wishes or procedures beyond that are purely up to the patient and family. One day when I woke from my day sleep, Linda told me that she had, in prayer, decided against any extra-ordinary measures to keep her alive. She said, "I will use my hands until I can't. I will walk until I can't. I will breathe until I can't." She asked for my support with her wishes. I agreed and found her stoicism to be amazing. I then had to pray that I would have the strength to go down this path with my beloved Linda.

Linda had several requests of me. She asked that I try to keep her in our home as long as possible. When the end came, she really did not want to go to the hospital or any other facility. She also asked that I agree to take her back to her beloved Nebraska for burial. She asked not to be cremated. She also asked me to reconsider my decision to be a full body donor to the State of Oregon. She said that she wanted me to be by her when my time came. At that time, I had signed up to be a full body donor when I died. I felt it was one last helpful thing I could do for society. I agreed to her requests and others that came up along the way. Fulfilling them was not always easy, but I would hope that whoever makes decisions about my end times will be respectful of my wishes as well.

She wanted to keep our day to day lives as normal as possible for the sake of Diedra, DaLyn, Jason, and Marci. She made a concerted effort to teach the girls about important things like cooking, gardening, and doing things right. We kept up our involvement in church and community activities as much as possible. Family still traveled to see us and we traveled to see them. I made the decision in 1994 to not seek another term on the La Grande School Board as already my time was being spent working and concern for the symptoms that Linda was having. I had served faithfully for eight years and I was satisfied with my service to the community in this way. I bid on a line operator job at the Boise Cascade Particleboard Plant where I was working. My seniority was sufficient for me to get the job. I had been working there twelve years and was just now getting the job that I always wanted at the plant. The line operator was in control of the entire production line. There was a lot of pressure but I felt that I was up to the task. I was still stuck on graveyard shift, but someday, if I stayed long enough, I could maybe go to day shift.

Almost every night before my evening nap before work, I would sit on the sofa and talk with Diedra and DaLyn about things going on at school and life. That was a great time and I often slept much better for my two-hour nap after sharing some "Dad" time with the girls.

On October 17 of 1997, my grandfather Sherman Stickney, the man who became my father figure when I was six years old, died of natural causes in Nebraska. He was eighty eight years old and had lived an amazing life of farming the land. He was very proficient at animal husbandry and was a role model for many in the small farming community which he lived. He was dedicated to God, family, the Masonic Lodge, and celebrating family history.

His ability to be innovative with repairing items was always amazing. Grandpa Sherm was always looking for a way to improve the process of whatever his interest was at the time. As a young married man, he and my Grandma Nellie followed the annual wheat harvest from Kansas to the Dakotas. The threshing machines that were used were not retaining the grain during the threshing process good enough. He developed a better internal separation process within the threshing machine. It was so well done that the John Deere Corporation gave him an award and he received a patent from the United States Patent Office. I remember working with Grandpa Sherm on the windmills on the farm to make them more efficient. This was done by better and permanent alignment and cutting down the resistance of the movement of the rod that connected the fan of the windmill to the wellhead. These are just some of the examples of the strength and depth of Grandpa Sherm's innovative mind. Most of the innovations were born out of the need for a repair and not having the money to buy new parts. Later in life, Grandpa Sherm discovered the many uses of a product called epoxy. Epoxy was a forerunner of super glue and Grandpa Sherm became adept at the applications of this product. He used epoxy to create small figures of people, animals, and other items for people to enjoy. For example, he took sea shells and made an entire family. He took pieces of corn cobs, grape stems, and little sticks to make a deer. While spending the winters in Arizona after retirement, he became a very good silversmith and jewelry maker.

One of our families most treasured items is a project that my Grandpa Sherm did in 1932. He carved a three-dimensional covered wagon and four oxen out of wood from an old organ cabinet. The wagon is fully functional and even has the large hand brake that the driver used to stop the wagon. Each ox is made from a solid piece of wood. The project took him all winter of 1932 to complete. This amazing art object has been on display in various museums and in his hometown of Ravenna, Nebraska.

The strength of character that he showed when most of his family was wiped out before his eyes in an accident, is legendary. Jason and I attended Grandpa Sherm's funeral. Linda was too sick to travel, and the girls stayed with her. Jason was one of the pallbearers and because he was still in the Navy, he wore his dress blues. At the gravesite and after the service,

Jason stood at attention at the head of the casket—a wonderful tribute to his Great-Grandpa Stickney. This would be the sixth tragedy in my life and the grace that followed it was that I eventually was able to help my Grandma Nellie (his wife of sixty-eight years) to have an estate sale in Nebraska and move to Oregon in 1999.

When Linda could no longer sign her name to checks and other documents, we had a signature stamp made for her to carry. It was notarized and legal for any document. Of course, her struggle with bi-polar disorder was still there and would rear its ugly head once in a while. I remember her asking the psychologist what she should tell people when they asked her what was wrong with her hands. He told her that they really do not want to know, so just tell them that the hands are not working too well. As time went on, the worry about bi-polar became somewhat tame as compared to the mental torture of ALS.

CHAPTER 26

GOING DOWN THE FINAL ROAD

The ALS started to affect Linda's legs in early 1997. We remodeled the house to add a large additional bathroom with a large shower that she could be wheeled into. We also added a redwood deck and ramp onto the side of the house. We could wheel her outside and she could enjoy the weather. She went with us to the store and church. We would put the wheelchair in the trunk and help her into and out of the car. At church we used the handicap ramp to take her—in her wheelchair—into Mass. Even though her mobility was declining, she wanted to—and we wanted her to—do all she could with us. She could go to school events that the girls had and we often went to the river or on a picnic.

Diedra and DaLyn took care of and assisted their mother in everyday tasks. She in turn would impart her wisdom on life and try to gently prepare them for the coming days when she would not be present. It was amazing to watch those two girls who were nine when Linda was diagnosed be so responsible for their age.

In July of 1998 Linda choked on a liquid she was drinking and aspirated badly. She had to be hospitalized for a short time and the decision was made that she should have a feeding tube inserted into her stomach for the delivery of water and nutrients. She had also lost so much muscle in her core that she could no longer sit in a wheelchair. The decision was also made to bring a hospital bed into the living room where she could easily be a part of the family activity. Our living room has a big 4' by 8' window that was wonderful for letting in light, and she could see the street, trees, and what the weather was doing. She was unable to take any solid food by mouth but once a week a Eucharistic Minister or Father Hank would come by and put a very small piece of the Holy Eucharist on her tongue. It would dissolve and that way she was able to still receive the Body of Christ. We got a baby monitor set: one monitor was by her, and the other monitor would be by my bed during the day while I slept. She could not really speak but she could make enough noise so that I could hear her through the monitor. At night, while I worked, DaLyn and Diedra would take turns sleeping on the hide-a-bed next to Linda's bed so they could help her if she needed it. Hospice came in once a week and checked on the feeding tube and any other medical needs. There was a wonderful group of ladies that came by every few days to spend time with Linda and to allow me to do errands and such. Linda's birthday was November 21 and the girls and I had a little party with her. DaLyn and Diedra's birthday was November 28 and we tried to celebrate but Linda was very weak. At this point she could roll one leg from side to side and she could blink her eyes—only. Hospice was coming every day now and on December 2, 1998 Father Hank came by to see Linda. He told me as we walked out that it would be a short time now. I had taken a few nights off work, so I was there for the 12:00 am feeding through the tube. Linda's breathing was very labored, and I sat on the sofa next to her bed. I was very exhausted at this point and I must have nodded off. I woke shortly after 12:30 am and the room was quiet. The love of my life, mother of my children, friend to all, and child of God, had gone home to her Heavenly Father.

Linda Louise Bernadette Miigerl Pokorney lost her three-year, nine month, and six day battle against amyotrophic lateral sclerosis at the age of 46 years, 13 days on December 3, 1998. I wept bitterly as I thought of the suffering that Linda had gone through. There were tears of relief also because that terrible disease did not have control of her anymore. She was home with God and I just had to be happy with that.

I called Hospice so that they could come and verify Linda's passing. Our good friends, Mike and Margaret Irish, came over to the house and Margaret spent time with the girls while Mike helped me when the funeral home came to get Linda. I had called Jason earlier in the day and told him that the end was very near. He was on his way home that night when I called to give him the sad news. Somewhere around daylight I laid down in my bed to sleep. Sleep would not come—just memories of Linda and the journey we had made together. I prayed that I would have the strength to raise DaLyn and Diedra as she would want. I vowed to myself that with God's help, this journey that had ended a life would not cause our family to be ripped apart. Just like earlier in my life when family and community made sure that two young boys would be taken care of, I made a similar vow now.

The next day the funeral home called and said that the Linda's body was ready for viewing. Only Diedra went with me as Jason and DaLyn were not ready for that next step at that time. When Diedra and I arrived, we went to the viewing room. The funeral director did not have Linda's hair positioned correctly. Diedra asked if he had scissors and he brought them to her. She put a tissue over Linda's face and cut her bangs so that Linda's hair style would be like she always wore it. That was a mighty grown up action for a thirteen-year-old girl. Diedra and I also noticed that Linda's hands were straightened out for the first time in about three years. It was a sign to us that the terrible disease of ALS had no more control over her.

A funeral Mass was held at the Our Lady of the Valley Catholic Church in La Grande on December 5, 1998 then I fulfilled another of Linda's wishes by having Linda's body transported to Nebraska for funeral and burial. A Rosary service was held on December 8 and the funeral Mass was held on December 9, 1998 at St. Mary's Catholic Church at Prairie Center. The church at Prairie Center is a country church just a few miles from Linda's home and is the church that she played the organ at when she was in high school. She was buried at our family plot in Ravenna, Nebraska. This would be the seventh tragedy in my life. The grace that followed it was that Linda was no longer suffering and that I was blessed with a son, daughter-in-law, and two daughters who were helpful to me. Together we moved on with our lives. Of course, the memory of our beloved wife and mother would and will forever be on our minds and hearts. I know not the reasoning of God, but I trust Him unconditionally.

CHAPTER 27

HOW DO WE GO ON?

DaLyn and Diedra were thirteen years old when Linda passed away. They were just three months into seventh grade and were attending the La Grande Middle School. I was still working nights and made sure the girls got off to school in the mornings before I slept. I was sure to be up in the afternoon when they got out of school, and if they had something during the day, I attended the event. Since we were all busy, we transferred our grief into hard work—nose to the grindstone kind of thing. Our dear wife and mother was always on our hearts and minds and she would want us to 'do things right' and not give up or give in to bad things.

Linda passed on to the children different traits and talents of hers. Diedra loved Linda's pies which were well known in the community and wanted to learn that skill. Linda taught her well and Diedra could make those pies just like her mom. DaLyn shared Linda's love of gardening and the knack of growing plants. She has the "green thumb" in the family and also is a skilled flower arranger. Jason inherited his mother's stoicism and resolve. Linda was a thinker and could think of different ways to fix something or handle a situation. Jason has that skill and I am often the beneficiary of his wisdom.

Still serving aboard the *USS Carl Vinson*, Jason made another western Pacific Tour in 1997. This time the tensions in the Persian Gulf region were high. We all watched the news intently, waiting for any news from that area. It is never easy being a military person and being away from home, but it is also hard to be the family that is waiting for any news. Many prayers were offered during this time and we always say a special prayer for our brave heroes that are serving around the world. Jason returned to the states and he and Marci lived in Oak Harbor, Washington, a beautiful area northwest of Seattle. Jason was stationed at the Whidbey Island Naval Station until his discharge in 1998.

Jason was now out of the U.S. Navy and he and Marci had moved to Meridian, Idaho. Jason was attending ITT Technical School and he graduated in 2001. He had acquired an interest in computers when he served in the U.S. Navy. When he came out of the U.S. Navy he wanted to get a degree in that field. It was nice that they were closer than they had been while he was in the U.S. Navy.

In the spring of 1999 the family and I convinced my Grand-ma Nellie that she should come and live in La Grande near me. She did not want to live with us, just close to us. First of all, we had to have an estate auction in Ravenna, Nebraska. It took five of us almost a week to get the auction ready. The turnout was massive, as we knew it would be. I will always believe that the attendance at the auction was more about the Ravenna community showing their love and respect to Grandma Nellie. The Stickney family had been solid residents for over a century and the community wanted to show their love. When the auc-tion was finished, DaLyn, Diedra, Grandma Nellie, and I drove back to La Grande. The grace of God was with us as a two-bed-room duplex became available right next door to my house. That meant that Grandma Nellie had her own place, but she was literally only twenty feet from my front door. The blessing of having Grandma Nellie living so close to us, was that she was able to share the wisdom of the aged to the girls and me. It was great to have Grandma Nellie so close, and as dementia would make her world very small later on, the girls and I were there to help. She enjoyed our visits several times a day and she looked forward to the "Meals on Wheels" deliveries.

Diedra and DaLyn moved on to La Grande High School in 2000 and were very active with studies, dance, and choir. In August of 2000, DaLyn and Diedra went to the World Youth Day in Rome, Italy. They went with the church youth group and had an amazing time seeing the history and culture of a different part of the world. They came back with a renewed love of the United States and the life we have here.

DaLyn and Diedra continued dancing with the Beckie Thompson Dance School and also danced with the La Grande High School dance team called Razz-Ma-Tazz. DaLyn danced until her senior year (eleven years) and Diedra danced until her junior year (ten years).

They also acquired after-school jobs at the Grande Ronde Retirement Center. Since they had been so helpful taking care of their mom, it was a natural fit for them. DaLyn worked at the main desk and Diedra worked in the dietary department. Diedra also played on the La Grande High School Girls Golf Team. She received excellent instruction from her coach, Mr. Lonnie Myers. She learned to love the game and played very well given the short time that she had been playing the game.

On September 11, 2001, Islamic terrorists used hijacked commercial airplanes full of people to use as flying bombs to attack the United States. Two planes hit the World Trade Center in New York City, one plane hit the Pentagon, and one plane crashed in the farmland of Pennsylvania. Over three thousand innocent people died. Diedra, DaLyn, myself, and the entire La Grande High School Choir were able to visit the World Trade Center site in New York City in 2004. The choir was on a performance tour and it was inspiring to hear those fine young people do an impromptu performance of our national anthem at that solemn site. I pray that the evil of terrorism can be eliminated from our world. I also pray that those young people who witnessed the horrible event on television will find a renewed sense of patriotism for the United States by visiting that hallowed site.

CHAPTER 28

GOD CHANGES MY LIFE
IN MANY WAYS

I had been overweight since graduating from high school. There were many overweight members of my father's family. I will always believe that my weight control and my offspring's weight problems are genetically caused. After moving to Oregon, I slowly gained a lot of weight. I reasoned that I was raised by very good cooks, married a very good cook, and was a better than average cook myself. I was a meat and potatoes eater. Sweets were never a problem for me. Instead of dessert, I would eat the last of the meat, bread, and gravy. I tried many diets and they would work for a while and then I was back to, or more than the weight I started at. I resigned myself to the fact that I would always be overweight and that I would try to make the best of it. My health did not suffer until about 1990. It was then that I was diagnosed and started treatments for

Type II diabetes, high blood pressure, and high cholesterol. I read an article about weight-loss surgery in 2001. I researched it more and found out that the success rate of certain types of weight-loss surgery was high. The problem was that my health insurance did not cover the $20,000 cost of the surgery.

One Sunday after Mass, I was talking to several friends and mentioned the research that I had done. A couple of weeks later a friend and his wife stopped by the house to deliver a Christmas card. It was then that God stepped in to the situation. My friends told me that if I believed the surgery would work, they would cover the cost. They insisted on no repayment and they wanted to remain anonymous. What a Christmas gift! God's grace at work.

I found a surgeon in Boise that had done many weight-loss surgeries and after an examination, he decided that I would be a good candidate for the Roux-en-Y gastric bypass surgery. I weighed 442 pounds when I went into surgery on February 2, 2002. The recovery was long and the adjustment by my body was very uncomfortable at times. As soon as I could, I started a very light walking routine to get my metabolism to kick-in and accelerate the weight-loss. In the first year I lost over 200 pounds. I am now, sixteen years after surgery, stabilized at a 130 pound weight-loss. All the medical issues I had before surgery are gone and I am sure that God, the surgery, my friends, and my resolve has given me more time on this earth to—do His will. I will be forever grateful to God who put my angel friends in my life. They were moved to help a man and family in need and I vow to repay them by doing good for others whenever I can.

On January 13, 2004, Jason and Marci became mom and dad to a sweet little girl named Delaney Jade Pokorney. She was the cutest granddaughter that anyone could have, and I was, and am, a proud grandpa. Delaney is a true gift from God as it was thought that Jason and Marci would not be able to have children because of a medical problem. They were married almost ten years when they were blessed by this wonderful daughter. It was wonderful that my Grandma Nellie was able to see and cuddle her great-great granddaughter.

DaLyn and Diedra graduated from La Grande High School in June of 2004. Their Great Grandma Nellie got to attend the ceremony and so did their niece. Both ends of the age spectrum celebrated with us all on that day. One who was not there in person was their mother Linda, but she was there in spirit and love.

In the Fall of 2004 I ran for a seat on the La Grande City Council and won. It was a four-year term and I believed that I had some insight in order to be effective for the job of city councilor. The La Grande City Council is made up of six councilors and the mayor. La Grande has a council/manager form of government which means that the city council hires the city manager and the city manager runs the day-to-day operations of the city. The city council's job is to set policy and ordinances for the city to operate efficiently. The terms of office of the council members are staggered so that there will not be a complete turnover in one election. The mayor is elected by the voters and only served a two-year term. The mayor can run for as many terms as preferred.

Jason and Marci both had full-time jobs and they asked Diedra if she would consider coming to live with them in Meridian, Idaho, to be a nanny for them with little Delaney. Everyone thought it would be a good idea, so Diedra went to be a nanny in the fall of 2004. She stayed on to help with the baby until the fall of 2005 when she returned to La Grande to attend the Future#1 College of Cosmetology.

In the fall of 2005, Grandma Nellie was not doing well. She was tired, the dementia made every minute confusing to her, and she would not eat. She took to her bed on October 31, 2005 and was semi-conscious. I checked on her often and called her doctor to see if there was something we could do. It was determined that she was slowly dying and that a hospitalization would not be helpful and it might make the time she had left worse.

On the morning of November 3, 2005, Nellie Stickney (she had no middle name) died with me by her side at the age of ninety-two years. Right before she died, she said that she could see her brothers Domie, Slim, and Martin and asked if I could I see them too. All of those gentlemen passed away many years ago. I said that I didn't but that she should keep watching for them. She then spoke the Polish language of her youth, which she had not done in a long time. She used to say that she had forgotten the language. I guess she hadn't.

This fantastic lady had a lifetime of hard work beside her husband Sherman. They met at a very early age and were inseparable for sixty eight years until he passed away. They worked in a timber camp in Northern Idaho, followed the wheat harvest from Kansas to the Dakotas, and owned and operated a wonderful and successful farm in Nebraska for forty two years. Grandma Nellie was a petite woman but for several years she picked corn by hand beside Grandpa Sherm for $1.00 per day. They witnessed the terrible loss of their only daughter, son-in-law, and two grandsons in an auto accident. They then raised the two remaining grandsons to manhood. I am one of those grandsons she raised, and I can tell you without a doubt that she is a saint. She was a fantastic cook (I know good cooks and she was really a great cook), seamstress, and was the cleanest person I have ever known. Her sewing ability was fantastic. She was obsessive compulsive before they gave it that name. Her sewing ability was fantastic. She and my mother Ruby Jeanne designed and sewed my mother's wedding dress from scratch. After leaving the farm she learned the art of stained glass and painting.

The loss of my Grandma Nellie would be the eighth tragedy in my life. The grace that followed it was that after losing her husband we gave her life a sense of purpose, by coming to live by the girls and me. She gave to us the wisdom of the aged and for the third time in her life, she became a mother-figure. This time it was for her Great-Granddaughters, DaLyn and Diedra.

DaLyn met a young man named Destry Anderson online and decided in December of 2005 to move to Coeur d' Alene, Idaho. It was hard to see her go, but most people leave the nest in order to find their dream. I did, and so it was with hope in my heart, a wish for good luck, and the words "You always have a home here" that she left.

CHAPTER 29

DAY SHIFT, MAYOR,
AND OTHER CHANGES

Jason had a two-year degree in computer science from ITT Technical Institute but felt that he needed more education in order to get a higher paying job. He looked at a lot of educational options for earning the final two years of his studies, when he would have a bachelor's degree in business. He and Marci decided that he would go the distance-learning route and do all of his work online. He enrolled with Colorado Technical Institute and started classes in 2006. Getting his degree the online way was not easy. It took a lot of personal discipline and he had to be committed to the studies. It is very easy to go do something fun, watch television, or sleep instead of studying. I admire Jason for having the discipline to complete his studies in two years. With that degree he was the first one in our family to have a four-year college diploma. My father William only had a two-year degree so that makes Jason the first with a four-year degree. Well done, Son!

In 2006, I finally got the chance to go to day shift and to keep the line operator job I liked the best. After twenty two years on graveyard, the difference in my sleep and overall outlook on life was completely different. Day shift was 7:30 a.m. to 3:30 p.m. During the summer getting off work at 3:30 p.m. was wonderful and there was so much daytime left that it was like having almost a whole day to do outdoor things. I had joined the La Grande Country Club around 1995 and now that I was on day shift there was a lot more time for golf. Diedra also played a lot of golf and she was very good at the game. Both of us had a lot of success at the game of golf and it was a real bonding time for Diedra and me.

Diedra graduated from the Future #1 College of Cosmetology in 2007. She worked hard to pass the courses in hair care, manicures, and pedicures. Before she could start working in a salon, she had to go to Salem for mandatory state testing and, because of her attention deficit disorder, we knew it would be a huge challenge for her. The ADD made tests and testing hard for her. She was so worried that I drove her to Salem and she studied all the way there. She would have me ask her questions and she seemed prepared. The testing was very rigid, as it should be when you are working with someone's hair and nails. We said a prayer in the car before we went into the testing office and Diedra was very nervous. I said more prayers while she was in the testing room, and when she came out she looked tired and defeated. We waited for a few minutes while the test was being scored. She said that it was hard, but she did the best she could. Diedra was called up to the front desk and the lady told her she had passed the test. Diedra literally grabbed the counter then turned towards me with a huge smile. I knew she had done it. We know that it was her hard work and study that gave the results, but I guarantee you that God had a hand in the victory too. God gave her the strength to do the study, take the test, and overcome a handicap.

When Diedra and I returned to La Grande from the testing she immediately started at a salon called the Main Attraction. She had known Anita Baker, the owner, for a while and Anita gave her a chance to start to build a clientele. Diedra loved her work and soon had a steady clientele. She liked working with the ladies that worked at Main Attraction but most of all she loved her clients. She would try everything in her power to meet their schedules even if it was late night or weekends. The salon was sold in 2013 and Diedra went to the Cutting Corner to work with Paulette and Tammy. The shop was smaller but again she loved the location and many of her clients followed her to her new work site. Diedra was very proficient at hair cutting and styling but her real talents were in her manicures, pedicures, and her fabulous nail art. She had the wonderful ability to paint designs, pictures, and multi-color designs on the nails of her beloved clients. Diedra loved her customers and even though there was a mix of political and social views, she tried hard not to judge others.

In 2008, my four-year term on the La Grande City Council was coming to an end and instead of running again for council, I decided that I would run for Mayor of La Grande. The incumbent mayor had been in office many years and I knew it would be an uphill battle. I did not win the election for mayor in 2008, but the count was close. Closer than most people thought it would be. I stayed very involved in city issues because I knew I would run for the office of mayor again in 2010.

When 2010 rolled around I filed to run for Mayor of La Grande. The incumbent mayor chose not to run for mayor but ran for a city council position instead. The election would pit me against a retired university professor, Mr. Doyle Slater. Doyle and I had known each other for many years and I respected his work: at the university, in the community, and for the LDS Church. The campaign was fun and we both ran for the position, not against one another. On election night the vote was close at each count. By about 1:00 a.m. the counting was over, and I was the new Mayor-elect for the City of La Grande. Home alone when the final numbers were in, I fell to my knees and prayed to God to give me strength and wisdom to be able to continue my long commitment to the community. I felt the weight of many on my shoulders, but I was prepared to follow-through on my visions for La Grande.

The next day at work there were many congratulations and many calls from community members wishing me the same. That's right: I still had a full-time job to do outside of being the mayor. I would not let down either my employer or the voters by slacking in either area. I resolved to work my hardest for the community and to be visible to the people. I took office in January of 2011.

I was fortunate to have some good friends who thought like me on the city council. One of the first items of business at that first city council meeting that I presided over was to not accept the small stipend that councilors and the mayor received. The money would be put in a fund and used to help organizations that needed a small amount of money to do a project. The motion passed unanimously. The next day the headlines read "La Grande City Council Gives up its Pay." Boy! That made me proud that our council would take a strong stance to help the community.

My dream for my term of Mayor in La Grande was to be a visible connection to city government. I made it known to organizations that I was willing to come to their meetings, special events, and any community sponsored events. I went to all ribbon cuttings and attempted to visit every business in the city to let them know I was willing to listen to their concerns. Some folks were initially skeptical of my motives, but soon they saw that I was sincere in learning all I could about everything in La Grande. I was still working full-time on day shift, so I often had two or three meetings or interactions each day between four o'clock and eight o'clock p.m.

I developed a wonderful working relationship with the city employees. Sometimes we disagreed on a vision or how we were going to get items finished but remained able to talk about the issues. Several of the department heads had many years of service which I respected. Since I had no direct responsibility for their performance, I generally and sincerely wanted to know their thought process to see how I could assist them.

In 2012 I had to decide whether to run for mayor again. Two years just had not been enough to see things accomplished, so I filed to run for another term as Mayor of La Grande. I had an opponent who was a friend and had different ideas of how the city should be run. Unfortunately, he passed away suddenly, just before the election. I missed his input on issues. He truly had what was best for the city at heart.

There was some changeover on the city council and getting to work with the new councilors was challenging but fun. I wanted to do an Economic Summit for the community to see where our strengths were and where were we falling short. A group of community folks helped make the summit happen and the response from the community was important.

Our local battalion of the Oregon State National Guard came home after being on deployment in Afghanistan. I was asked to make a speech for the demobilization ceremony. As the father of a veteran, it was very meaningful to speak to our returning heroes, their families, and community folks all assembled at the football stadium. Their sacrifice is supported and honored by small communities like La Grande.

I believe that the legacy that I left to local government was that elected citizens should be visible and involved with the community they serve. Yes, it takes time and effort to build a reputation for being a listener to concerns. When that listening takes place and action is added, then that builds the public trust and leads to true representative government.

CHAPTER 30

ANOTHER ADDITION TO THE FAMILY AND MY COMMUNITY SERVICE IS OVER

DaLyn Elizabeth Francis Pokorney and Destry Jon Anderson decided to get married in Coeur d' Alene in August of 2013. Diedra would be the Maid of Honor and Delaney would be a junior bridesmaid. Destry's mother owned an old church that had been converted into a wedding chapel. It was a beautiful and stately building in the old part of Coeur d' Alene. I was honored to walk DaLyn down the aisle. She was a stunning bride. The reception was in the basement of the wedding chapel which was wonderfully decorated for such events. Dalyn's aunt and uncle from Nebraska attended and we were so glad that they made the trip to represent Linda's side of the family. Linda was certainly there in spirit, and we all wished DaLyn and Destry a long and happy marriage.

In March of 2014 I decided not to run for another term as mayor. I have described in chapter 1 my reasonings for stepping aside and to re-iterate, I felt that God was telling me that He had other missions to attend to. I did not know what those would be, but again I listened and waited for the Lord to lead me. It is not easy to wait on God. We, as humans, sometimes think that we know best and that we are the god of ourselves. Only through prayer and patience can we truly receive the correct message from God.

In August of 2014, I had some chest pains one day at work. I finished out my shift and then had a meeting with some members of the community. The pains did not go away and only got worse. I excused myself from the meeting and went to the Emergency Room at the Grande Ronde Hospital. I was admitted to ICU and the next day I had a stress test that indicated that I had a blockage with the blood flow around my heart. I was flown by Life Flight to Boise for evaluation from a cardiologist. I was taken into an operating room and the doctors performed an angiogram and then did an angioplasty to break up the blockage. The recovery went well, and I missed very little time from work.

The work at my employer, Boise Cascade, was increasing and there were many opportunities and a need within my job classification to work overtime. I took the opportunity that presented itself and worked many twelve-hour and some sixteen-hour shifts. I was already contemplating retirement and knew that the extra funds would come in handy.

So, the last city council meeting took place in January of 2015 and my overtime hours were increasing at work. I was now seriously researching my retirement date with Social Security and the Boise Cascade pension fund. I decided through prayer and adding up the numbers that March of 2016 would be my retirement month. The date was one month after I turned sixty-two years old and was the fortieth anniversary of my hire date with Boise Cascade. Through the years I have seen friends and co-workers work for a few years after they were able to retire for various reasons. Many times, however, something happened, and they died before enjoying their retirement years. I vowed that, if I could afford it, I would retire as soon as possible. I had no big plans but wanted to have whatever time that God granted me on this Earth, to be mine and not be tied to a job. My health was relatively good, but for the last year or so I have been noticing a mostly subtle, yet sometimes a not so subtle loss of memory and increased anxiety. I told my employer that I would be retiring on March 19 of 2016.

CHAPTER 31

MY HEART IS BROKEN AND MY LIFE WILL NOT BE THE SAME

Diedra had been having trouble with her tonsils for several months. She went to the doctor and he reported to her that her tonsils were very large and if not removed, they would affect her breathing and sleep. She had already been having trouble with sleep and she had a hard time singing, which was one of her loves in life. She played guitar and sang at the Saturday evening Mass at Our Lady of the Valley Catholic Church and enjoyed it a lot.

I advised her that she should have them removed because I had my tonsils removed when I was forty-two years old and everything went wonderfully. I told her she would feel much better and that the recovery would be fairly short. I could tell she was apprehensive and she seemed to have a fatalistic view about the surgery. She went through all the preliminary testing and all indications were positive for a successful procedure. Unknown to me she had conversations with her twin sister about what her final wishes were if something went wrong in surgery.

She checked into the hospital on November 2 for the surgery and I was with her. Everything was still a go as far as the tests and the doctor were concerned. She was nervous, so I tried to reassure her that all would be okay. Diedra lived with me and I told her that she would have all the right soft foods and that I would take good care of her. The surgery lasted a little longer than the doctor had thought, and he reported that he removed the largest set of tonsils that he had seen. He called them "award winning." Diedra stayed in the hospital two days and then came home. She was very uncomfortable and could not sleep in her bed, so she slept in a recliner here at home. On the third night she woke me up and she was bleeding badly and was scared. We called the doctor and he said to meet him at the emergency room at the hospital. After an examination he said that he would have to put her back into surgery and re-cauterize the wound site. Again, all went well, and I took her back home. She slowly improved but was impatient about the recovery. Diedra went back to her work at the salon on a part-time basis on or about November 12. She resumed full time work on November 18. She had an appointment with the doctor and he said that the healing was proceeding on schedule. On Friday November 20, Diedra complained of being short of breath. I told her that it was just because she was maybe overdoing the work. Since she was a very big lady, she was often short of breath anyway. Saturday November 21 was the anniversary of Linda's (Diedra and DaLyn mom) birthday. This next paragraph is so hard to write. I must write it however no matter the pain.

The morning of Sunday November 22, 2015 was cold and a little snow was on the ground. I got up and showered, shaved, and dressed for Mass. Diedra had told me, before she went to sleep, that she wanted to go to Mass with me on Sunday November 22. She was still sleeping in the recliner as she felt she was breathing better than when sleeping in her bed. I was sitting at my computer and was checking my e-mail when she woke up and walked by me headed to the bathroom. About five seconds after she went by me I heard a huge crash in the bathroom. I went in to see what was wrong and Diedra was lying on the floor on her side. I called her name but there was no response. I tried to turn her over to get her into a seated position. She was still breathing but not conscious. I called 911 and tried to get her to come to. The paramedics arrived and they came into the bathroom. She was propped up against the door that went into the other bathroom. The EMT tried to awaken her as I was holding her with my arm around her back. She opened her eyes, looked at me, and said "Dad" in the way she always did when she wanted my attention. I said, "I'm here," and she opened her mouth to take a breath, went limp, and her eyes rolled back. My precious daughter was gone.

The EMTs then took control and they asked me to leave the room. They started CPR and various other procedures. I had not realized it, but there were now four EMTs and two police officers in the house. I knew all of these fantastic gentlemen and they tried so hard to save my Diedra. They put a CPR cuff around her body, put her on a gurney, and took her to the hospital. One of the EMT's whom I know very well looked at me when they were leaving, shook his head and grabbed my arm. I said, "I know Stan, I know." At the hospital a full team worked for about a half hour trying to get any kind of vital signs. The total time elapsed since she had spoken my name was now about forty-five minutes. The doctor came out to the waiting room and said that they had not had any success in reviving her. I told him to stop the process. I knew she was gone. They let me go back and see her and I fell apart, much like I am doing right now.

Diedra Marie Therese Pokorney is gone. She was twenty-nine years old and just six days shy of being thirty years old. She was strong in her own way and received joy from helping others. Diedra could bake great pies and loved family time the best. She was a beautiful singer and loved to entertain. She was disorganized but seemed to always know where something was if it was important. Diedra had a heart of gold, but if you crossed her, she could "bulldog up" with the best of them. She was a natural leader with a take charge attitude.

As hard as it was to have my daughter die in my arms, the next task was just as bad. I had to call Jason, her brother, and

DaLyn, her twin sister, and tell them that Diedra had passed
away. Both of them, after the shock subsided, said that they
would be home ASAP. I called my friend Kevin Loveland at
the funeral home and asked him to take care of Diedra for
me. I was driving home in a daze and the next thing I knew I
was parked at the church. Early Mass was just getting out and
I went in and told my friends and Father Saji Thomas what
had happened. It was wonderful to have them show their love
for me and sadness for the loss of Diedra. Shock was evident
among our friends at church. They all had known Diedra since
birth, many were her clients, she had provided their music at
Mass, and they all were immediately supportive of me.

I got home and in this house I never felt so alone. I was
heart broken as I re-lived those moments when she called my
name and looked at me for help. I couldn't help her. Nobody
could. Then the questions started. What caused this? What
could be so serious that she died so quickly. I remembered
her mom and the long goodbye we had with her illness, but
Diedra was up and walking and in a few minutes was gone. I
realized that I had to inform family in Nebraska about what
had happened. How was I going to tell them? The questions
they would ask about what went wrong, I had no answer for.
After I called the family, I put a post on Facebook that Diedra
had passed away and the messages of shock and support came
flowing in. It would be a while before Jason and DaLyn could
get here, so I was alone. Or was I? Amid all the mind-numbing

questions and the "what do I do now" thoughts, there seemed
to be an inner strength. Yep, God was in control. He had let
me, and He had made me, hold my daughter in my arms while
he took her to His home. I wanted answers but God wanted me
to wait until it was His time.

The funeral director called and asked me if I wanted an
autopsy done. I said absolutely not. He said, "Daniel, you and
the family are going to want to know what caused this sudden
death." He also told me that if the District Attorney ordered
an autopsy, it would be out of our hands. I asked why such an
order would be given. He said because it was a sudden and
medically unattended death of a young person. Within an hour
the autopsy was ordered and I was furious. I felt that Diedra,
the family, and I were being violated. The paramedics who had
been here to help had left some items and they stopped by to
get them. When they came here to the house they had two grocery sacks of food items. What a great crew they are and what
a great community to be in.

Jason, Marci, and Delaney arrived first and it was so good
to have their love and support. DaLyn and Destry arrived shortly after and we were together as a family. We were however, a
family painfully missing a mother who had been gone seven-
teen years and daughter/sister who had just left us. The pain
of tragedy is overwhelming. The love of God our Father is the
only way to successfully deal with that pain.

CHAPTER 32

ANSWERS AND TRIBUTES

More phone calls needed to be made, Flowers had started to arrive here at the house. The next day DaLyn, Destry,
and I went to the funeral home to make the arrangements.
While we were talking about the arrangements, the funeral
director received a phone call, which he put on the speaker
phone, from the Medical Examiner in Portland, Oregon. She
had finished the autopsy and reported that the cause of death
was massive pulmonary embolisms (blood clots) throughout
Diedra's body. We learned later that the clots were caused
by a fairly rare medical disorder called disseminated intra-
vascular coagulation (DIC). DIC can be caused by the blood
chemistry getting out of whack after a surgery. The body,
as it is trying to replenish the blood supply, gets the chemistry wrong and too much coagulant is made. That causes
the blood clots. The symptom is shortness of breath (which

Diedra had) and is rarely diagnosed before death occurs. So now we knew.

We went to the church to plan the funeral Mass and to the cemetery to find a good spot for Diedra's final resting place. We found a plot that is near the top of a hill. It has a beautiful panorama of our beautiful La Grande and the mountains surrounding it. Every time I go there (which is very often) the beauty always amazes me. It is amazing that God finds a way to soften the blow of loss by using little things to give us peace in our hearts. Because of the upcoming Thanksgiving holiday (November 26), and the birthday of Diedra and her twin DaLyn (November 28), we planned the Rosary for November 29 and the funeral for November 30.

The day of the funeral was cold and windy. The Rosary had been attended by many people. In a special tribute, Nancy, Carolyn, and Ron, former choir mates, sang a song around Diedra's casket. The funeral Mass was at Our Lady of the Valley Catholic Church. The same church where she first went to Mass, received the Sacraments, and served her fellow parishioners with her music ministry. We were happy that my brother David came from Colorado and that DaLyn's friend Jo De came from Coeur d' Alene. Loveland Funeral Chapel livestreamed the funeral service so that all the family in Nebraska could watch the funeral without worrying about the bad roads and weather. I stood at the church doors and greeted folks as they came in. My heart was overfilled with joy and gratitude that so many people would come out on a cold Monday to be there for Diedra and the family. DaLyn and I had picked out the recorded music that we liked and one of the songs was by Diedra's request. She had told DaLyn that if something happened she wanted the song "The Dance" by Garth Brooks to be played. You bet we did. I had asked eight of my wonderful friends from the Knights of Columbus to be the pallbearers and they responded amazingly and with strength. As I said earlier, Diedra was a big lady, and my friends handled her with care and respect. I read a poem that I had written for Diedra and when I looked out on that absolutely full church, I thought, "they are all here for you Diedra."

The ladies of the parish put on a wonderful dinner after the funeral and burial. My granddaughter Delaney put together a wonderful slide show of pictures and memories that ran during the dinner for folks to see and remember our dear Diedra.

So, this would be tragedy number nine. The grace that followed had several layers. Diedra was financially responsible, so left a fairly easy estate for me to settle. She did not have a lot of debt and I passed her car on to my granddaughter Delaney. Diedra was so looking forward to my retirement and she wanted me to enjoy "my" time. For the most part that has happened. I just wish that Diedra, Linda, my Grandpa and Grandma Stickney, my mom, dad, and brothers could be here to enjoy it with me. God, you have this, and I trust in your ways.

CHAPTER 33

RETIREMENT AND ANOTHER FAMILY LOSS

On March 19, 2016, I officially retired from Boise Cascade Corporation after forty years of employment. In those years I saw the best of times and the worst of times in the wood products industry. I worked with good and talented people and I worked with bad and lazy people. I had good supervisors and terrible supervisors. I had friends in higher level management and I had higher level management that disliked me and tried to get me fired numerous times. Through it all, I believe that I gave the company the best I had. I did entry level jobs, dirty jobs, routine jobs, and jobs with a tremendous amount of responsibility. The company in turn, gave me respectable pay and benefits. They also provided a pension plan that, hopefully, will sustain me until I die.

After retirement, I had several items around my house that I wanted to get to and worked hard to make that happen. I was able to finally read many of the books that I had wanted to read, but never had the time. My good friend Al told me about a free audio book lending system through the La Grande Public Library. It is called OverDrive and I have used the service a lot. The variety of books is wonderful and it is super easy to access. My friends Al and Colleen MacLeod own a coffee shop in downtown La Grande called Joe Beans Coffee. It is a very friendly place and I enjoy going there in the mornings to visit with folks. There is a core group that are there on a regular basis and we are joined daily by others who enjoy a great cup of coffee, a delicious pastry, and lively conversation. Dick, Ken, Byron, Jean, Mike, Jeff, Ted, and others are the regulars. I treasure their friendship.

I am not much of a traveler, but I did go to Wyoming in 2016 to research the accident that took the lives of four of my family. I have traveled to my home state of Nebraska each year to visit friends and relatives.

In early April of 2017, my daughter DaLyn called me with some exciting news. She and Destry were expecting a baby. She was happy, and I was happy for them. On Easter Sunday, April 16, 2017, Destry called me and said that DaLyn was very sick and that he was taking her to the hospital. We weren't sure what was wrong at the time, so I packed a bag and left immediately for Coeur d' Alene, Idaho to be with them and help in any way I could. It is a four-hour drive. When I arrived DaLyn was in tremendous pain, both physical and mental. The doctor had said that there was a problem with the pregnancy. Early the next day she was taken into surgery and they found that the pregnancy had been a tubal pregnancy. The tube had burst, and the doctor was unable to save the baby, but the doctor felt that DaLyn would be okay. Because DaLyn had only one ovary as a result of an ovarian cyst earlier, and now the tube to the remaining ovary was destroyed, this young couple would be unable to have children naturally.

This would be the tenth tragedy in my life and the grace is that while the baby was lost, the doctor was able to catch the problem early enough so that DaLyn would be okay.

The eleventh tragedy happened on June 6, 2018. My father-in-law, Paul Eugene Miigerl, passed away at the age of ninety two. He had been in failing health for several years after a lifetime of farming and ranching. Paul was a man of faith and a man who had many talents. After his semi-retirement from farming he took up woodworking. He was masterful at the wood projects. Virtually every member of the family has a piece of woodwork that Paul crafted. He made large furniture items as well as much smaller items. Gardening and baking cookies were other examples of Paul's talents. Paul's dedication to his Catholic faith was very strong and he was an inspiration to me in many ways. Paul's funeral was truly a celebration of the long and successful life that, with faith in the Lord, he lived to the fullest. Paul was a veteran of World War II and was honored at his funeral with full military honors. The grace that came from Paul's death was that he touched many lives in a positive way during his life and leaves an extended loving family to carry on his legacy.

CHAPTER 34

FINAL THOUGHTS AND UPDATES

An update of family members is as follows. My brother David and his wife Kathy live in Pagosa Springs, Colorado. David is retired and is battling several health issues. Kathy is the Assistant Superintendent at a school on the Apache Reservation. My daughter DaLyn and her husband Destry live in Coeur d'Alene, Idaho and have quite the menagerie of pets. DaLyn works for a home care organization as a care coordinator and is the "green thumb" of the family. Destry is a U.S. Army veteran and deals with a disability but has a variety of interests. My son Jason (a U.S. Navy veteran), daughter-in-law Marci, and granddaughter Delaney live in Meridian, Idaho. Jason is a network engineer with Stability Networks in Boise. He is a great cook and enjoys making new dishes. Marci is a trainer at the Alaska Airlines Call Center in Boise. She is a great wife and mom who deals with the effects from rheumatoid arthritis (RA). Delaney is an amazingly talented incoming freshman at Meridian High School. She is a drummer and also a long-time Irish dancer. My mother-in-law, Adella, lives in a retirement facility in Kearney, Nebraska. My late wife Linda's three sisters and their families all live in Nebraska. The extended family is very important to me. They have always been there with support and prayer. Through the magic of the internet, I am pleased to be in contact with many relatives, high school classmates, and friends. Each and every one of those contacts are a connection to the past and mostly happy times.

I remain a passionate man about my love of the United States of America and the beautiful Constitution that the founding fathers wrote, with the help and guidance of God. I am a strong voice for conservative values and I have a profound respect for life, from conception until natural death. I believe and support small businesses as they are the backbone of the economy of the United States.

One last item. In December of 2015 I was diagnosed with early onset alzheimers disease (ALZ). It was diagnosed through a battery of tests. My neurologist is a good friend and he is helping me through this time. I was starting to see and feel the signs in early 2014. I thought it was the stress of work, politics, and impending retirement. The effects lessened a little when I retired from work and politics but I now am feeling increased anxiety, the misplacement of items, and forgetfulness.

So, I guess that this is the tragedy number twelve. The grace is God has seen to it that I should write this book before any more of my faculties are lost.

God has led me down this path, fraught with pain and loss, to strengthen me. God also gave me times of extreme joy and gladness. After each of the painful episodes, the Lord gave me the grace to move forward. The graces were not always immediately evident but, in due time, I came to see them in my life. Whatever lies ahead for me, it is God who will make the calls. God has truly written this book. I pushed the keys, but He put the words on my mind in order that everything hopefully makes sense. All praise and glory to God for my life up to now and however long this journey may be.

Please, I want the reader to know and understand that I am not the hero in this story. Through all these tragedies I have had weak moments. Times of crisis of faith and the always present—"why me" thoughts creep into my mind in those quiet and lonely times. The blessings of the Father, however, brings me back to a level of understanding that provides the strength needed for me to move on. My ultimate dream is that I will be welcomed into His presence, see my loved ones again, hear God say, "Well done faithful servant."

ACKNOWLEDGMENTS

To **God**—for staying with me in good times and bad times. I am not a perfect man, but my faith in you gives me hope to see you face to face in heaven.

To **my lost loved ones**—within me resides the strength that each of you instilled in me. You showed and taught me (most times I didn't even know it) the way I would travel. With each of you in my heart, I move forward.

To **Jason Pokorney** and **DaLyn (Pokorney) Anderson**— (my beloved adult children)—you are always there for me and you believed in me and this book. Thank you for helping me remember stories, dates and details. This book is your heritage.

To **family and friends**—thank you for encouraging me and having helpful suggestions. So many of you have offered prayers for me and for the completion of this book.

To my editors **George Venn** and **Mary DeViney**—your expertise really helped me get this book to be presentable to the reader.

To my graphic design expert **Nancy Allen**—This book will be enjoyable to the reader because of your terrific talents. God sent you to assist me and you accepted the challenge flawlessly.

To my spiritual advisor **Zee Koza**—You know me so well and are truthful in your advice and counsel. We have been down many roads together and your gift of friendship is treasured by me.

To my publisher **Kristin Summers**—Thank you for helping to make a first-time writer's dream come true.

ABOUT THE AUTHOR

Daniel S. Pokorney is a retired millworker whose life has been rocked by episodes of tragedy. Through it all he eventually saw and experienced the grace of God following each tragedy.

This book project was in the planning stage for about five years. On Easter Sunday of 2018, Daniel felt compelled by God to start the book. The book was finished in 56 days and it is Daniel's belief that God wrote the book, he merely pushed the keys on the keyboard.

Daniel's many years of community service includes eight years on the local school board, four years on the local city council, and four years as the Mayor of La Grande, Oregon, a city of 13,000. This is Daniel's first book.

www.facebook.com/tragedytograce

For more information or to order additional copies, please visit:
www.TrilliumMemoryBooks.com/tragedy-to-grace

Also available through Ingram, Amazon.com, Barnesandnoble.com,
Powells.com and by special order through your local bookstore.